Improvisation with Favorite Tales

Improvisation

with Favorite Tales

INTEGRATING DRAMA INTO THE READING/WRITING CLASSROOM

Ruth Beall Heinig

HEINEMANN
Portsmouth, NH

Heinemann
A division of Reed Elsevier Inc.
361 Hanover Street   Portsmouth, NH 03801
Offices and agents throughout the world

Every effort has been made to contact copyright holders for permission to reprint borrowed material where necessary, but if any oversights have occurred, we would be happy to rectify them in future printings of this work.

Library of Congress Cataloging-in-Publication Data
Heinig, Ruth Beall, 1936–
    Improvisation with favorite tales : integrating drama into the reading/writing classroom / Ruth Beall Heinig.
        p.   cm.
    Includes bibliographical references.
    ISBN 0-435-08609-X
    1. Language arts–Study and teaching (Elementary)–United States–Handbooks, manuals, etc. 2. Drama in education–United States–Handbooks, manuals, etc. 3. Tales–Study and teaching (Elementary)–United States–Handbooks, manuals, etc. 4. Activity programs in education–United States–Handbooks, manuals etc.
I. Title.
LB1576.H332   1992
372.6'044–dc20   92-519
                                                                      CIP

Designed by Jenny Jensen Greenleaf.
Printed in the United States of America.
94 95 96   10 9 8 7 6 5 4 3

CONTENTS

PREFACE

The use of children's literature in the classroom is growing at an unprecedented rate. Many teachers have embraced the philosophy of literature-based teaching, incorporating numerous selections in their language arts program, of course, but using them as the focus of other curricular learning experiences as well. Even in classrooms where traditional basal readers are used, teachers are seeking out supplementary reading materials to augment the children's literary experiences.

Fine literature mirrors life and provides material for a variety of language and learning experiences. It introduces readers to the emotions, conflicts, questions, and ambiguities of everyday life. Readers create meaning from literature on the basis of their own life experiences and understandings. When reader and text meet, a new experience is forged that becomes part of a reader's total being, to be reflected on again and again.

As well as expanding their use of literature in classrooms, educators are increasing their repertoire of techniques to encourage children's responses to literature. Some responses are written: stories, diaries, news articles, or letters. Other responses are oral: conversations or group discussions. Still other responses include movement, the visual arts, music, or drama.

Dramatizing literature in the classroom provides students with an effective and pleasurable way of exploring both the world and themselves. Through drama, children are required to examine a story more closely, improving their comprehension and understanding. They are encouraged to think creatively and pretend to be their favorite characters, examining life from various viewpoints. When literature from other cultures and times is introduced, children gain global and historical perspectives. And, because drama is a group art, children learn to engage in productive social interaction, cooperative learning, and group problem solving.

Drama capitalizes on a child's natural urge to play with literature. Young children, for example, spontaneously take part in stories that are read or told to them. They chant along with the "trip trap" of billy goats going over the bridge, or join in the bear's query, "Who's been eating my porridge?" Their bodies sway to rhythmical passages, and they may even act out the hero or heroine's movements as their imagination is captured by intense, dramatic passages. Even though older elementary students are more restrained as an audience when listening to stories, at the mention of acting one out they excitedly exclaim, "I want to be the wolf [or the queen or the peddler]!"

Several favorite stories, mainly folktales, provide the basis for the various drama activities in this book. This type of literature lends itself well to dramatization because of the boldly drawn characters and active plots. Some of the activities presented are derived directly from the stories. Other activities go beyond the story line, introducing new characters and situations that encourage children to speculate creatively and to invent ideas, thereby exploring the basic story in greater depth. And, for each story, a "Related Activities" section suggests additional responses in areas such as writing, art, and music.

It is hoped that these stories and the activities presented here will assist teachers in their attempts to make drama and literature come alive in their classrooms.

INTRODUCTION

How to Use This Book

Those of you new to drama will want to study the "Drama Activity Components" and "Specific Activities and Techniques" sections before trying any of the story activities. If you're a seasoned drama practitioner, you may feel comfortable proceeding directly to the stories and activities, referring to these introductory sections as questions arise.

Each story section begins with a plot summary of the most common telling of the tale. If students are not already familiar with the story, you should read it to them. In most cases a number of picture book versions are suggested. Many have been recently published and are handsomely rendered. The illustrations should enhance the imagination and provide numerous details for discussion and elaboration as you begin the dramatizations.

For each story you will also find a listing of additional resources. For the most part, these are retellings or variants from other countries and cultures. Sometimes they include humorous or satirical takeoffs of the commonly known versions that are well worth sharing with the children. These variations have helped inspire many of the "beyond the story line" activities presented and should give you and your students further ideas to explore.

You will need to be the final judge of which of the stories and activities presented here will work best with your particular group. While folktale literature is suitable for virtually all ages, some stories in this text are traditionally associated with certain age levels. "The Three Little Pigs," for example, particularly delights five- and six-year-olds, while the Norse myth "The Search for Thor's Hammer" can probably be best appreciated by middle to older elementary students.

Another consideration to keep in mind, however, is that the drama activities created for each of the stories range from the fairly simple to the more sophisticated and complex. For the youngest elementary children, you might use primarily the easier activities that adhere to the original story line. Many young children are very literal about their favorite stories and are puzzled or disconcerted with variations or deviations from traditional plot lines. On the other hand, many equally young children have a rich literary background and are able to appreciate story variations, even contributing some of their own ideas.

For middle and older elementary children the simpler activities can serve as warm-ups to the more challenging activities. These children will enjoy the activities that go beyond the original story line, taking new twists and turns, even if the stories are generally associated with younger children.

If you teach drama exclusively, this book should still provide useful exercises for all your classes, since the tales are universal and were originally told to multi-age audiences.

You are definitely encouraged to experiment with, change, or adapt the activities in this book to suit your needs or those of your students. Furthermore, the techniques and ideas presented are intended to be models for additional experimentation. For example, many of the activities suggested for one story will work equally well for other stories in this book or for stories not included here. (Even your students will quickly see the variations that are possible!) Finally, as you work with these activities, you will see ways to incorporate them into your total curriculum, using characters and incidents from all subject areas. Only by making your own explorations and modifications will you be taking full advantage of the ideas presented here.

Drama Activity Components

One of the biggest concerns beginning drama leaders have is classroom management. A basic understanding of the underlying structure of drama activities should alleviate this concern and enable you to choose or design appropriate activities with greater confidence.

One way to approach drama activities is to identify some of their basic components, keeping in mind the question, what will this activity require my students to be able to do? Look at the drama components listed in the two columns below. Each component in the left-hand column has a corresponding component in the right-hand column. As a general rule, the components in the left-hand column are considered easier than those in the right-hand column. Therefore, if a drama activity contains one or several of the components in the left-hand column, it will probably be easier for children to play than if it contains one or several of the components in the right-hand column.

Easier Components	More Challenging Components
pantomime	verbal activities
solo work	pair and group work
desk space	larger areas of space
unison playing	playing for observers
directed playing	creative playing

Let's examine each of these components in more detail.

Pantomime   is the performance of dramatic action without using words. Much of the plot line of any given piece of literature is expressed in action. Specific characters' actions also move the story forward. These actions provide the basis for many pantomime activities.

Pantomimes are fun for all children. Young children in their pretend playing do an incredible amount of mimed action; they usually feel very comfortable with pantomimed pretending and engage in it easily. Although older elementary children can perform pantomime fairly easily, some may initially need a little encouragement. At least one reason for this is that school structure tends to confine older children to their desks so much of the time that they are surprised when pantomime is suggested as a viable activity. They may also sense a little embarrassment, because pantomime movement draws attention to bodies that, in many cases, are going through rapid and uncomfortable changes. But the fun of the activities soon helps them forget these concerns, and they play as easily as when they were younger.

Verbal Activities   include a wide range of vocal experiences, from creating sound effects to improvising short scenes. Verbal activities are considered more challenging because many of them require a certain sophistication in the ability to manipulate language. Younger elementary children can be successful with many of the verbal activities presented in this text if you make allowances for their level of development. (Surprisingly, some very young children can engage in rather sophisticated discussions when the topics are suited to their level of expertise.) Older elementary children usually excel in verbal activities, since their verbal skills are more highly developed. Often they will sit at their desks for extended periods contentedly speaking in character or discussing issues and problems related to the characters in the stories.

Solo Work   means that each child participates singly rather than interacting with others. For pantomime solos the entire class frequently plays in unison, with children staying at their desks or in their individual spaces. This eases classroom management. If more space is needed, a few children can play at a time, while the others observe. Or you might divide the class in two groups and let one half play while the other half observes.

Another thing that makes solo activities, both pantomime and verbal, easier to do is that they can usually be played rather quickly. Everyone has the opportunity to try out an idea briefly. This chance to experiment is also helpful to you as the leader, because you can test out topics and ideas and measure the children's interest in going further.

Younger elementary children particularly enjoy solo pantomime work because they all get to play a character immediately, eliminating competition for roles and waiting their turn. For older children the activities can serve as warm-ups to the more challenging ones.

Paired and Group Work is considered more challenging than solo activity because it requires interaction and some basic skills in cooperation. When children pantomime together, for example, their movements usually have to be coordinated in order to produce a meaningful message. When children engage in dialogue, they will need to take turns, compromise, integrate ideas, and use other social skills. Because of the interaction required, paired and group activities generally take more time to plan than solo activities.

As a general rule, because of their greater developmental level and experience, it is easier for older elementary children to engage in paired and group work; younger elementary children will be challenged by it. Although younger children can be introduced to simple paired and group activities early on, they will need more direct guidance to play them successfully. Expectations for them should not be as demanding as for older children.

Group work is generally most successful when there are no more than five persons interacting. With five, the group cannot divide itself into two equal factions. Groups may be made larger in inverse relation to the difficulty of the task being assigned. For example, if children are to arrange themselves into a "frozen picture," they can probably work in larger numbers than when they are asked to improvise a scene together. Needless to say, the larger the groups, the greater your need to give careful instructions and assistance.

Desk Area Using the children's desk area for playing is easy and convenient. Furthermore, it is an important management strategy. Children automatically tend to be quieter, and idle chatter is reduced, when they are seated. The desks also help maintain order by creating a concrete boundary for children who have difficulty exercising self-control. Working in the desk area also helps shy children feel more secure because it provides a safe haven from which to express themselves.

A desk need not be solely restrictive, however. It can become a useful prop in the drama by serving as a car, a horse, a bed, or a throne. Even locomotor actions such as walking or running can be performed at the side of the desk—"in place."

Desks are also convenient and useful places from which to engage verbal activities in pairs and small groups. For paired talking, children can simply face the person sitting next to them. For small-group discussions, desks can be clustered together.

Larger Areas of Space Using larger areas of space will require more classroom management skills on your part and more adherence to rules on the students' part. Experienced leaders know the problems involved in getting children just to rearrange the classroom desks quietly. Through experience, you will learn not to be afraid to make rules and hold your students to them. After all, children won't really have fun in drama if there are no controls.

More space will usually be required for paired and group playing and for activities staged as scenes, especially if movement is involved. A number of management hints and techniques are suggested throughout this text to assist you if you are taking your first drama steps.

Unison Playing In unison playing the entire class performs simultaneously, with no one being the center of attention and no audience of peers observing. The playing may be solo (without interacting) or in pairs or small groups. Unison playing is considered easier than playing for observers because the focus is on the participants. Unison playing also aids children's concentration and involvement in their work. Obviously, shy children are more comfortable playing in unison than in front of an audience. Eager, outgoing children also enjoy unison playing because they don't have to wait for a turn to get involved.

Playing for Observers means that an informal audience of peers is present. The goals here are more challenging since they involve sharing ideas with others, communicating interpretations, and garnering feedback for one's messages and thoughts.

There are a variety of ways to structure an audience. At the most basic level, children may simply enjoy watching their classmates while waiting for their own turn to play. At a more involved level (pantomime guessing games, for example), the audience is required to interpret the performers' actions, decoding their nonverbal messages. Finally, an audience may also be asked to evaluate classmates' ideas and interpretations.

Shy children often need to move gradually into playing for observers, requiring quite a bit of encouragement along the way before they feel comfortable. Conversely, outgoing children are sometimes more motivated to do well when they know someone will be watching them. The latter will need help and guidance to become more inwardly motivated, learning the joys of playing for their own satisfaction instead of being engaged only when an audience is present.

Directed Playing   means that you as the leader tell or coach the children in fairly specific terms what they are to do. This is considered easier for children since they are required to do very little creative thinking. Take the following pantomime solo, for example:

> *Pretend you are a small seed. First, curl up on the rug. As I count, you will grow up slowly until you are standing tall and in full bloom when I say five. Ready? One . . . two . . . etc.*

The directions for the pantomime are simple and straightforward. Even the youngest child should be able to do it. There are clear-cut cues for moving and stopping. In addition, the slow movement should help children focus their concentration and stay on task.

Creative Activities   are more challenging, since they require varying degrees of inventive thinking. Often these activities go beyond the given story line. Note the following prompt for a verbal solo:

> *Goldilocks, what are you going to tell your mother if she asks where you've been all day?*

This question requires a child to take on the character of Goldilocks, interpret her feelings, and speculate on an idea not answered in the story. Other creative activities might be:

> *In pairs, one of you be Rumpelstiltskin spinning the straw into gold while the other creates the sound effects.*

> *In your groups, plan a different ending to the story. After you've planned and rehearsed, we'll watch you act out your ending and then discuss your ideas.*

Both directed and creative activities serve important purposes and neither is necessarily superior. The directed activities are usually simpler for children to do; in fact, some children need the guidance and structure that directed activities present. Creative activities call for inventiveness and give more responsibility to the children. Children will probably be more successful with creative activities when their imaginations have been nurtured over time. They will also need the feeling of emotional security triggered by your accepting responses in order to be at their creative best.

Organization of This Book

The activities for each story in this book are grouped as follows:

1. Solo pantomime activities (no interaction with peers).
2. Solo verbal activities (interaction may be with leader).
3. Paired and group pantomime activities.
4. Paired and group verbal activities.

This arrangement is designed to help you select and sequence your activities: the activities that are generally easier are listed first, followed by those that are more demanding. The solo activities generally may be played at the desk, while the paired and group activities generally require more space and interaction with peers.

It is not necessary to play all the activities listed for a given story nor must you play them in the order presented. Instead, you may select freely, using the activities that appeal most to you and to your class and are most appropriate. Of course, your choices will also depend on the amount of time you have available. Many of the more challenging activities, such as improvised scenes, will take quite a bit of time to plan and play, perhaps more than a single class period. You may even let some children select appropriate activities for independent work to be shared with the class at a convenient time.

Another alternative is to select one activity from each of the four groupings under a given story to structure a drama lesson. This technique will ensure some variety in the lesson and will include both easier and more advanced activities.

As the children try out the various activities, they may express an interest in staging a play from them. In this case, you might arrange the activities in chronological order and create your own informal play. The activities thus serve as rehearsal units. Although not all the scenes of the story are included in the activities, there are enough to form a skeleton framework for creating a play. (If you use this technique, the activities that go too far beyond the story line will probably have to be omitted.)

Finally, be sure to encourage the children's ideas for other drama activities. Once you—and they—feel comfortable with the format used here, you should be able to create your own activities and dramas with any piece of literature you choose.

Specific Activities and Techniques

Most of the drama activities in this book have specific names. The activities and the procedures for playing them are described in detail below, arranged alphabetically under the headings "Pantomime Activities" and "Verbal Activities."

Pantomime Activities

Build a Place   In this pantomime game children, using gestures only, create an imaginary room or space and equip it with appropriate furnishings or objects. First, you as the leader mark off the corners of a playing space on the floor, perhaps nine feet by twelve feet. (You may use chalkboard erasers or masking tape.) Then the doors or entryways to the space need to be marked. (These may be mimed, if you like. For example, a doorway might contain a regular door, French doors, a sliding door, draperies, etc., each of which would be mimed in a different manner.)

The players pantomime bringing in suitable objects and placing them in an appropriate spot. Large or heavy objects like a sofa or a long table may be mimed by players in pairs or even threesomes. After each item is placed, the observers guess what it is.

For older elementary children you may create two doors or entryways, one at either end of the space, thus giving more children a chance to pantomime. Guessers also have more people to watch.

As an added challenge, once the first item is placed, players bringing in a new item may be asked to *use one of the previous items in some way*. The objective is to ensure a lasting image of the created environment. For example, two players bring a sofa into a living room; the next player brings in a rocking chair. After placing the rocking chair, the player may rock in it for a few moments and then go to the sofa and sit before exiting. Periodically, you or the children should review all the items in the room and their placement.

At first, children will need help remembering to walk through the entryways instead of the walls. After a while, though, they will get very adept at this game; in fact, the illusion of the imagined space will become so real you may want to end the game very deliberately. You might ceremoniously "erase" the space, miming with a chalkboard eraser in the air; or you might pretend to fold up the room and place it on a "shelf," promising to bring it out again in the future. With experience, children will also become more sophisticated about the items they deal with, cutting holes in the wall for windows, constructing a fireplace, or even installing a light switch.

Count/Freeze Pantomime   In this pantomime guessing game, several children simultaneously each act out his or her individual idea in front of the class while you count from one to perhaps ten and then say freeze. The audience then guesses what the pantomimers were performing. As each child's idea is guessed, he or she sits down. By having several children at a time pantomime their individual ideas, the entire class has an opportunity to play in a reasonable amount of time. This is considered solo playing since there is no interaction.

However, the count/freeze pantomimes may also be played in pairs or even small groups if the idea you are working with lends itself to that approach. In this case, the game is considered paired or group playing.

To make the game easier or to control the topics chosen, you may have the children draw cards with ideas written on them. *Hint:* Don't let the guessing go on endlessly. If an idea cannot be identified in three guesses, the pantomimer(s) should simply tell what was being done.

Fast-Motion Pantomime   This is, obviously, the opposite of slow-motion pantomime (see p. 12). Double or triple time is another way of expressing it. Fast motion can be dramatically effective in showing urgency or portraying mechanical actions. It can be a useful exercise in achieving control. Because it encourages children to think quickly and act rapidly, it can help hide fears shy children may have about performing the actions. It is also a useful way to work off children's excess energy, preparing them for a more quieted and thoughtful activity.

Frozen Picture   Children, in pairs or small groups, are given a scene to depict and asked to freeze in appropriate positions. Children may also select their own scenes to portray to be guessed by the rest of the class.

Variation: Frozen scenes may be performed as shadow pictures or silhouettes. Use a bright light (a clamp-on floodlamp serves well) behind a taut sheet in a darkened room. Children need to stand close to the sheet in order to present the clearest outline. Colored gels on the light can create interesting effects.

Improvised Scene   After some initial drama experiences, children are usually ready to try an improvisation. This is a scene from the story, involving two or more characters, that is either pantomimed or played with dialogue. At this point, we will consider just pantomime scenes. (See p. 15 for a discussion of an improvised scene that incorporates dialogue.)

Scenarios, or simple plot outlines, may be suggested. For example, an improvised pantomime scene might be:

> *Let's see the scene when Hansel and Gretel leave their home with their parents and then become lost in the woods. The scene will end when they find the witch's house.*

If the children seem to need assistance now and then with a pantomime scene, you may interject some sidecoaching (e.g., "And then the queen tiptoed to the window . . . ").

Variation: Divide the class into small groups and give each group a scene to present. The groups usually need to rehearse for a few minutes before sharing their ideas with the class. As they gain experience and confidence, children may ask to enact their scenes without any rehearsal. They like the challenge of thinking on their feet and not knowing what others are going to do ahead of time.

Intragroup Pantomime   This game provides a good way to use the art of pantomime for brainstorming ideas. It is probably too complicated to be played by children under the age of eight.

The class is divided into groups of five or six. Three members of each group are pantomimers and the others are guessers. A topic is given, such as: "Act out all the words you can think of that begin with the letter *S*." As rapidly as possible, the pantomimers, without conferring with each other, pantomime their ideas for the guessers to guess and record. Both the pantomimers and the guessers are allowed to pass if they wish to give up on a word that cannot be guessed. When it looks as if the pantomimers are running out of ideas, end the game and compare listed ideas.

Hint: To avoid competition, give each group a different topic.

Mechanical Movement   Moving in a mechanized way is a good exercise for developing self-control and also great fun for children. They may move individually (as a robot) or work in pairs and groups (as a complex machine with various moving parts).

Mirroring   For this activity, two children face each other. One pretends to be looking into a mirror; the second child becomes the mirror, duplicating the actions of the first. The object is to align the actions so closely that an observer finds it a challenge to tell the "real" from the "reflection." At first it is easier to perform the movements in slow motion so the players can get used to following each other carefully.

After children gain experience mirroring in pairs, they can begin mirroring in small groups. Various situations can be used. For example, a salesclerk might help a customer try on an article of clothing. These two are mirrored by two others for a total of four players. Another player might be added to the scene as a tailor taking measurements for alterations; when this person is mirrored, the group totals six.

Narrative Pantomime   Some literature has enough action in it that you can ask the children to pantomime selected passages while you read them aloud. Usually the best material for this purpose has one character, though sometimes there may be two people or even a small group. There should be no (or very little) dialogue.

Often it is helpful to have the students listen to the passage or activity first so they will know what they will be doing. Some elaboration or editing of the text may be needed to make the action flow smoothly.

You can also build on action in the story and create your own brief narratives. For example:

> *Be Jack climbing the beanstalk. Stand at the side of your desk and begin climbing higher and higher. Look down and see that your house is just a tiny spot on the ground. . . .*

In addition to describing action, narrative can relate sensory experiences (sight, sound, taste, touch, and smell) or reveal feelings and emotions.

Noiseless Sound　Many vocal sounds (e.g., shouts, cheers, coughs) can be indicated without making any noise. An added challenge is to mime them in slow motion. This exercise is amusing to watch and is very good for encouraging disciplined movement. Children can quickly see the delightful results of slow, thoughtful movement.

Pantomime Solo　In this activity you ask the children to mime an idea. As stated previously, pantomime solos are most frequently played by all the children, each at his or her own desk or area. For example:

> *You are Snow White making a new suit of clothes for one of the dwarfs. Let us see what part of the outfit you are making by the way you hold and work with it. Remember, the dwarfs are small.*

Often it is necessary to give specific signals to start and end the playing. For example, you might use a visual cue (flicking classroom lights) or an audible cue (drum, tamborine, bell). You may also count to signal the playing. For example, if you have three ideas you want the children to enact, say:

> *Think of three things Goldilocks might have done while going through the woods and number them one, two, and three in your mind. As I count, you will play each of your ideas.*

Such cues are extremely important for keeping all the children on task and working together. It cannot be overemphasized that taking a little extra time to cue carefully will contribute immensely to the children's success in playing.

Pantomime Spelling　This pantomime game can be challenging and works best in grade three and above. In it, words are spelled out by the same number of children as there are letters in the word. Each of the players pantomimes an idea (in a given category) that begins with his or her letter. For example, the name of a character—troll—is spelled out by five children who have selected the category "occupations." They line up in the correct order and simultaneously pantomime:

T-eacher; **R**-ace Car Driver; **O**-rganist; **L**-ibrarian; **L**-ifeguard.

Other categories for these pantomimes might be verbs (action words), sports, animals, foods, emotions—anything that can be easily described through actions.

Before the pantomiming begins, two clues are given to aid the guessing. In the example above, the clues would be:

- This word is a character in the story.
- The category is occupations.

As the players pantomime, you as leader count (the same procedure as that used in the count/freeze game). If the guessers are allowed to use pencil and paper, they can solve the word as if it were in a crossword puzzle (i.e., they can often guess a word without knowing all the letters).

To make the game easier, have the children draw idea cards or brainstorm a list of words that could be used. You can make this a good cooperative learning activity by asking the guessers to work in groups, accepting an answer only if it is given by the entire group.

Quieting Activity   This type of activity is specifically designed to help children calm down after active playing. It is particularly useful at the end of a session, but may also be used intermittently as needed.

Sidecoaching   Like an athletic coach, you as the drama leader may offer verbal suggestions or encouraging comments to the children from the sidelines in order to heighten and advance the playing. This is called sidecoaching.

You may also sidecoach by noting what the children are doing. This recognizes individual work (without using specific names) and is a way to suggest ideas to those who might need additional help. For example, suppose you have asked the children to be farmers working in a garden. As sidecoaching, you might say:

> *I think I see a farmer hoeing some weeds; there's a farmer planting some seeds; and I believe I even see someone tasting some of the crops. Good work!*

Another way to sidecoach is to play appropriate music to fill in the "awkward" spaces. Establish a cue such as, "When the music begins, you will begin playing; when the music ends, you are to stop."

Slow-Motion Pantomime   As the name suggests, this activity is played slowly and deliberately. Children are usually familiar with slow-motion movement because they see it frequently: televised sports replays, demonstrations of astronauts moving in an antigravity environment, and time-lapse photography.

Most children will need encouragement and sidecoaching (see above), however, in order to achieve flowing and disciplined movements. Usually they have a tendency to speed up unless they are constantly coached to move slowly. Playing slow background music and coaching with a very slow rate of speaking also helps. ("T a k e i t e a s y. S l o w i t d o w n.")

Many groups will take a while to develop skill in slow-motion movements, so be patient. Over time, their skills will grow and the effort will have been worth it. Children will be very pleased with their accomplishments and often take great pride in performing slow motion effectively.

Statue   In this activity, individual children become a person or object in a frozen position. Guessing may be incorporated into this game unless the statue's identity is obvious.

Variation: Groups may also be in statue positions, as in frozen pictures.

Transformation   In this activity, children become people or objects that change magically from one thing to another. An example would be Cinderella's pumpkin changing into a grand coach. A transformation may be played solo or in pairs and groups. It is more effective, and children's concentration is deeper, when the transformation is made in slow motion or with appropriate musical accompaniment.

Tug of War   Two teams face each other. They pantomime holding a rope taut and, on signal, pull in an imaginary tugging contest. You as the leader may pretend to be a sports announcer and coach the event. The highlight is to allow the rope to break, followed by a slow-motion fall on the count of ten.

Verbal Activities

Conversation   Children are paired or grouped as characters in the story. They talk with each other about a given topic, expressing feelings and thoughts appropriate to their characters. These conversations can take place simultaneously for a brief period of time (from thirty seconds to perhaps two minutes).

Afterward, if desired, conversations can be presented to the whole class. *A good technique for sharing:* Select perhaps five pairs (or small groups) who volunteer and number them one through five. They can either go to the front of the classroom or remain in their seats. Call their numbers randomly and let them speak for a few moments so the class can hear at least a portion of their conversations. Repeat until all pairs and groups who wish to have shared. This is a quick way to satisfy the desire to perform.

Variation: Here is an added challenge for older or more experienced children. After one pair or group has spoken, the next players must *carry on* the conversation begun by the previous speakers.

Debate   In a debate, children argue opposing points of view. For example, in the story of Cinderella, the two stepsisters could argue about who is wearing the prettier ball gown. Or the prince may want the ball to be held on Saturday night while his parents think a weekday is a better choice. Or one of the rats doesn't want to be turned into a horse, and the fairy godmother has to use persuasive tactics.

The easiest way to conduct a debate, and one that works well even with young children, is to divide the class in half and assign a role and viewpoint to each side. Call on a volunteer from one side to give a reason for his or her stand, then call on a volunteer from the other side to respond, and so on. You may even list the points that are made on the chalkboard for further study and comparison.

Sometimes it is helpful if you moderate the debate by playing the role of an impartial character. For example, in the situations cited above, the stepmother might listen to the stepdaughters' arguments; a royal party-planner would be interested in the date of the ball; and Cinderella herself would be concerned about the fairy godmother's success in convincing the rat to cooperate. As you listen to the children debate, you can comment very briefly, the way your character might, on the points being made. "Mmmm, I hadn't thought about that." "Ah, yes, interesting observation." "Oh, dear, this is so complicated." You may even make a point or two of your own or ask further questions.

Variation: Older or more experienced children may be allowed to debate in pairs privately, making a list of the important points to be reported afterward to the whole class. An advantage to this approach is being able to air more ideas quickly.

Variation: Debates can also be presented as performances, using the same procedure described under "Conversation." In addition to having pairs debate, you can expand the scene to four people, with two on each side of the argument. A scene with six should have three people on each side, and so forth.

Variation: Cast a panel of perhaps six or eight characters, equally divided, to speak to two sides of an issue. For example, several members of the three little pigs' family could believe it's important to build a house cheaply and quickly; an equal number of family members feel sturdy construction, though expensive, is the best investment. The audience is allowed to ask questions of the panel members in order to explore the various viewpoints. The audience may also play character roles. In the above example, they might be other farm animals who have questions or their own divided views on home building.

Whatever method of debating you use, it's a good idea to let children switch roles whenever possible. This gives them the chance to become familiar with both sides of an issue. It is interesting to see how often new ideas come forth when children are suddenly "on the other side of the fence." Another good learning device is to ask the children to come to a mutually agreeable decision, a challenge that encourages the pursuit of compromise.

Experts   This is a panel game in which several children volunteer to be experts on a subject you assign. They sit in front of the other class members, who question them on their area of expertise. You as leader moderate the questions and answers, perhaps in the manner of a television talk show host.

You need to design inventive topics for your experts; the children need to be able to voice their own ideas and opinions without knowing specific information. For example, the experts might be inventors of a new and unusual product like a magic wand. Whatever ideas they have on making magic wands can be accepted, since there is no known or preconceived approach.

Imagination Game   In this game, you show interesting objects, props, or bits of costume to the group, asking the children to:

a. Guess who owned or used the item;

b. Think of new uses for the items; or

c. Demonstrate using the item as a certain character might, perhaps even making a comment as that character.

For example, if the item is a stovepipe hat, a child might envision its being worn by the wolf in the "Three Little Pigs." He or she might put it on and say the huff-and-puff line. Incidentally, garage sales and kitchen shops are excellent sources for these kinds of items. Children like to bring in their own items, too.

Improvised Scene   After some initial drama experiences, children are usually ready to try an improvisation. This is a scene from the story, involving two or more characters, in which the dialogue is made up as the players enact the scene.

Scenarios, or simple plot outlines, may be suggested. For example:

Let's see the scene where one of the little pigs meets the person with building materials. How quickly will the little pig decide what he wants? How much persuasion will be needed?

Encourage the players to say the dialogue in their own words. You might discuss the scene beforehand by asking, "What do you think the little pig might say to the person selling the straw?" As children become accustomed to improvisations, they usually like to go ahead without discussion.

If improvisations are new to you, treat them as experimental exercises. For example, you might say to the children, "Let's just try this and see how it goes." This open, accepting attitude will help the children risk something new. And it will relieve your anxiety about the outcome, too. Remember that the fun of improvisations is spontaneity. No one knows exactly what will be said—just as in everyday life!

It is also best to call on those children who seem ready and willing to participate. Shy children learn from watching their bolder peers and, in time, will gain the confidence to try it themselves. Giving a good deal of praise and encouragement to the players also helps.

Variation: Call out "freeze" during the scene and choose new volunteers to continue the same scene. This procedure allows more children an opportunity to play and lets everyone see the various interpretations players may have of a character or situation.

Variation: Divide the class into small groups and give each group a scene to present. The groups usually need to rehearse for a few minutes before sharing their ideas with the class. As they gain experience and confidence, children may ask to enact their scenes without any rehearsal. They like the challenge of thinking on their feet and not knowing what others are going to say or do ahead of time.

Interview   An interview may be conducted in a number of ways. Children may be paired or grouped. One plays an interviewer, newspaper or television reporter, police officer, or other legitimate questioner. Whenever possible, allow the children to switch roles so they can experience both asking and answering the questions.

Paired interviews may take place simultaneously, with the children noting things to discuss afterward in the larger group. Interviews may also be shared with the class as described under conversation and debate.

Note: Many of the solo verbal activities in this book suggest that you as the leader play an interviewing role with the entire classroom. These activities can be changed to paired interviews, if you prefer. Again, this procedure saves time and provides more opportunity for children to present their ideas, especially if the entire class wants to talk at once. (You'll know when you see their hands waving furiously in the air!)

Interview Panel   A panel of people may be interviewed by the rest of the class. For example, several children all pretend to be the gingerbread boy and take turns answering questions from the audience about their thoughts, attitudes, or motivations.

Audience members may also play a role. For example, the audience collectively may be reporters or citizens who ask questions appropriate to their role. Audience members may decide their own roles and even give themselves specific names or occupations, identifying themselves before asking their questions.

I'm the little old woman. Why did you run away from home?

I'm the baker in town. How does it feel being a cookie baking in an oven? Was there a special ingredient in your dough that made you come alive?

Variation: Panel members may each be a *different* character in the story, answering questions from the audience relevant to their specific characters. Thus a panel might consist of the gingerbread child, the old man, the old woman, and the fox. Again, audience members may play roles as well.

Leader in Role   In this activity, you pose as someone other than yourself in order to stimulate discussion and thinking among the class. The type of role may vary considerably. You might pretend to be a person who is helpless and in need of assistance. Or you might play an authority figure who is in command and can give orders. The character may be from the story or one appropriate to it.

While in character, you may present information through messages, letters, decrees, proclamations, or other documents prepared beforehand. You can also use props to stimulate further ideas and discussions. An intriguing box, an ornate key, a curious picture, and so forth are useful for such purposes.

In playing a role, you *suggest* the character rather than *become* the character as an actor might. There is no need to perform in a stereotyped or showy manner; simply speak the words the character might say. For example, as Cinderella's stepmother, you might say,

Cinderella, I told you to scrub the floor. When I tell you to do something, I expect it to be done.

While you would speak these lines with emphasis, it isn't necessary to take on a sharp, shrill voice and exaggerated movements as a stage actress might. The dialogue usually delineates the character sufficiently. By taking on a role in this fashion, you can play a wide variety of characters, even those of the opposite sex or persons significantly different from yourself.

Note: If a role seems unreal or phoney, you can present the idea in a letter from that person. You might pretend to be a friend of the person, acting as a messenger. This is also a useful technique if your character (such as a witch) would be too scary for little children.

To set yourself up in a role situation, you may simply announce, "Now I'm going to pretend to be the queen." Or you might say, "I'm going to leave. When I return, I'll be someone else. You'll know who I am by what I say." Then, simply turn your back for a few seconds, face the students again, and speak as your character.

Another useful strategy is to let the children carry on their discussion and decision making without your character's presence. This technique works well if your role is viewed as somewhat threatening or if you think the children would feel freer discussing their ideas "in private."

After your "character" leaves, you can:

1. Return as teacher and monitor the children the way you normally would.
2. Return in a different role, perhaps the same role the children are playing, and add your own thoughts legitimately to the discussion.
3. Sit on the sidelines and let them work independently until they appear ready for your character's return.

Sound Effects   Sound effects can be created in a variety of ways. Sometimes excerpts from a story can be read and sounds made on cue. The volume can be controlled by using a "sound indicator": a cardboard or wooden arrow, an oversized pencil, or a ruler. As you move the indicator up or down, the sound increases or decreases. When you turn the indicator horizontally (to the "off" position), the children must be silent.

Sounds can be made with voices, with objects in the classroom (e.g. a pencil tapping on a desktop), or with musical instruments. You might even wish to tape-record the sounds for children to hear in playback.

Sound Mime   This is a pantomime performed by one or more persons to the accompaniment of appropriate sounds made by another person or group. Those making the sounds must match the pantomime. For example, a pantomimer knocks at a door; the sound of the knocking is made by the sound-effects players.

Variation: Reverse the game by having pantomimers match their movements to the sound effects. For example, the sound of knocking is heard; the pantomimer must provide an appropriate action such as knocking at a door or answering a door.

Storytelling   Storytelling may be anything from a lengthy explanation of events to an original story complete with a beginning, middle, and end. The story may be told by an individual or a group. For round-robin storytelling, each child contributes a sentence or two, adding on to the previous tellers' ideas.

Storytelling Through Sound   This activity is a more sophisticated version of sound effects. A story may be told, in outline form, with sound explorations. The sounds may be made vocally, with simple musical instruments, or with found objects.

For example, the story of Hansel and Gretel may be outlined as follows: Hansel and Gretel are lost in the woods; they discover the witch's candy house; the witch appears suddenly; Hansel and Gretel are imprisoned; Gretel triumphs over the witch; Hansel and Gretel are reunited with their father.

Appropriate sounds are discussed and planned by the group, interpreting the events in a variety of ways. To indicate the discovery of the candy house, children might decide to include some ooh's and aah's along with munching and satisfied lip smacking. To indicate the witch's sudden appearance, there might be a poof sound followed by cackling. Older children may use more abstract sounds, simply indicating the emotion of the moment, perhaps with musical instruments.

Children may work on the sounds as an entire class, or they may be grouped and assigned to be in charge of specific scenes. Allow them enough time to experiment with various ideas and interpretations. When everyone is satisfied, you (or a capable student) can then conduct the brief sound piece as an orchestra conductor would, cueing in the various groups when it is their turn.

Verbal Solo   For a verbal solo, you as the leader pose questions to the class as a whole, often assigning them a particular role (e.g. "Cinderella, what do you think about . . . ?"). Children may raise their hands and be called on, one at a time, to engage in a brief conversation with you.

For some verbal solos, you may play an interviewer such as a reporter or police officer or anyone else having a legitimate interest in the information. Other questioning roles can be drawn from appropriate characters in the story.

Usually it is best to call on volunteers rather than force children to talk. Shy children often first need to hear their peers responding before they develop the courage to speak up themselves. However, you can *invite* quiet children to give their opinions or ideas as a way to let them know their contributions are valued.

If all the children seem eager to speak, you can simply go quickly around the room and give everyone a chance to voice an opinion. To save time, you may stipulate, "Tell me in just one sentence."

If your students are talkative and find it difficult to wait their turn to speak with you, you may pair them up and have them tell each other their ideas. If they can talk quietly, the entire class can participate at the same time. Ring a bell (or use another definite cue) to signal when you want them to begin and end. Another alternative is to change the activity to an interview panel (p. 16).

Who Am I? Selected players pretend to be certain characters and are questioned regarding their identity. The only questions allowed are those that can be answered yes or no. Establish a limit of perhaps twenty questions that may be asked. Audience members may guess the identity of the character(s) any time they think they know. However, if a questioner gives an incorrect guess, he or she is eliminated from that round.

Final Note

An adage in the theatre states, "Always leave them wanting more." This is a useful rule to remember when conducting any drama activity. It is not necessary to exhaust everyone's ideas before ending. Instead, move to another activity shortly after children peak in their creative flow and excitement. Topics can always be returned to at another time.

The Story of The Three Bears

AN ENGLISH FAIRY TALE

Summary: *When three bears decide to take a walk and let their morning porridge cool, a little girl wanders into their home and creates mischief. She eats the porridge, accidentally breaks a chair, and falls asleep in the baby bear's bed. When the bears discover her, she is so frightened she jumps out the window and runs away.*

Selected Picture Books

Goldilocks and the Three Bears. Retold and illustrated by Jan Brett. Dodd, Mead, 1987. Lavish detail, medieval designs, and intricate borders are presented in this version.

Goldilocks and the Three Bears. Retold by Armond Eisen and illustrated by Lynn Bywaters Ferris. Knopf, 1987. In these illustrations, Goldilocks is a pretty child in Gibson-style dress.

The Three Bears. Written and illustrated by Paul Galdone. Ticknor & Fields, 1985. Realistic-looking bears and a mischievous-looking Goldilocks with missing teeth characterize the pictures in this version.

Goldilocks and the Three Bears. Written and illustrated by James Marshall. Dial, 1989. With wit and humor, Marshall tells the story in his inimitable style.

Related Sources

Little Bear's Sunday Breakfast. Written by Janice. Lothrop, Lee and Shepard, 1958. Little Bear visits "her" house in this turnabout tale.

Goldilocks. Adapted by Tom Roberts and illustrated by Laszlo Kubinyi. Rabbit Ears, 1990. Illustrations of a turn-of-the-century southern setting and dialogue filled with quaint country sayings give a new twist to the old tale. Goldilocks is also a bit of a snob: she says "Who is their decorator?" upon entering the bears' home and notices that the sheets on the beds don't match.

"Goldilocks and the Three Bears." Written by Roald Dahl. From *Roald Dahl's Revolting Rhymes.* Knopf, 1983. The poet thinks Goldilocks should be tried for her crimes, not the least of which is not removing her dirty shoes before getting into bed!

"The Grievance." Written by Sara Henderson Hay. From *Story Hour.* Doubleday, 1963. Goldilocks has been adopted by the bear family, but the baby bear can't forgive her for her transgressions.

Solo Pantomime Activities

Pantomime Solo

• You are Goldilocks. Suppose you are interested in all animals' homes. Let's also suppose that you visit some of those animals' homes before you find the bears' house. As I count to three, you will investigate three possible homes of other animals. On the count of four, you will reach the home of the three bears and sit at the breakfast table.

Narrative Pantomime

• You are Goldilocks walking (*in place*) through the woods swinging your long, golden sausage curls. They're especially bouncy today and just right for showing off. Skip through the woods. Now run. Now, sit down on a large stone and rest yourself. My, how exhausting it is to be the center of attention!

• Be Goldilocks tasting each of the three bowls of porridge—the big one's too hot, the middle one's too cold, but the little one's just right, so you eat it all up. You try out the chairs—the big one's too hard, the middle one's too soft, but the little one's just right, except that the bottom falls out and down you go. Now you're so tired you go upstairs and try out the beds. But the big one's too high at the head; the middle one's too low at the foot; the little one is just right, so you cover yourself up and fall fast asleep. Pleasant dreams!

• Each of the three bears and Goldilocks eat porridge in a very different manner. Let's see what those differences are, remembering that the bears are "well brought up" while Goldilocks is not. First be the great big bear (Papa), then the middle-sized bear (Mama), now the little wee bear (Baby), and finally Goldilocks.

Solo Verbal Activities

Verbal Solo

- We think that Goldilocks might have been sent on an errand, but we don't know what the errand was nor who sent her on it. Is there anyone here who can answer both questions for us? Tell us who you are and how you know this bit of information.

- You're one of the three bears. Tell us what you did on your outing in the woods while you were waiting for the porridge to cool. The way you answer and the voice you use should let us know which bear you are.

- Baby bear cried when he saw his chair broken. But, then, baby bear often cries at the least little thing. You are baby bear. Crying again? What is it this time? (*You as leader respond as mama or papa bear.*)

Paired and Group Pantomime Activities

Count/Freeze Pantomime

- Goldilocks probably spent a lot of time wandering around in the woods before going to the bears' house. Several of you will act out something you think she might have done. The rest of us will guess.

- What are some of the things the bears might have done on their walk in the woods? Show your idea in groups of three for us to guess.

Build a Place

- Besides the bowls of porridge, the chairs, and the beds, what else do you think a family of bears would have in their house that was so intriguing that a little girl would go in uninvited? Build that house and include the items Goldilocks was attracted to.

Frozen Picture or Improvised Scene

- (*Divide the class into groups of four.*) Create the scene in which the three bears discover Goldilocks. Make sure we can tell which bear you are.

- Show the three bears at home [or on a picnic, shopping, doing house chores, at the zoo, etc.]. Be sure to show what each one might be doing so we can see what their individual interests are.

• Create the scene in which the three bears are cleaning up the mess that Goldilocks left behind. Baby bear should be able to help, too, although his parents will have to guide him. As the music plays, in your groups of three you will put the house back in order again.

Paired and Group Verbal Activities

Verbal Solo

• (*Divide the class into three groups and assign big, middle, and wee bear roles.*) The bears love to sing. Remembering what your different-sized voices are, let's sing "Mary Had a Little Lamb."

Storytelling

• Suppose the story of the three bears was turned around and baby bear is the one who pays a visit to Goldilocks' house. How might this story be told? (*Afterward, the children might like to hear the story* Little Bear's Sunday Breakfast, *listed above.*)

• The neighbors often swap stories about the mischievous adventures Goldilocks gets herself into. She is definitely not the sweet little girl she first appears to be! What stories are they telling about her today?

Experts

• According to some versions of the story, Goldilocks was not a well-brought-up little girl. Today we are fortunate to have some specialists on manners who will answer our questions about how well-brought-up children are supposed to act in different situations.

Interview and Leader in Role

• Suppose Goldilocks left before the three bears came home. When the bears discover the damage in their house, they call the police. In groups of five, two officers will questions the three bears. What questions will the detectives ask in order to gather their data? Is it possible that the bears themselves left the house in a bit of disarray? Besides the food that was eaten, the broken chair, and the mussed-up bed covers, what other evidence is there that someone was in the house? How do you conclude that it was a little girl? (*After the groups conduct their interviews, you as leader play the police captain and compile the reports from everyone. For younger children, this activity should be done in pairs—one detective and one bear.*)

Improvised Scene

- Goldilocks returns home after being gone for several hours. Her parents are worried about where she's been and angry that she's been gone so long. They demand an explanation. What does Goldilocks say and are her parents satisfied with her story? (*Do this in pairs or groups of three.*)

- The bear family, who never even locked the doors in the past, decides to install a security system. Two salespeople for the security company call on the bears to sell them a system customized for their home. What security devices will the salespeople try to sell and what will the bears decide to order?

- Baby bear has decided he's getting too big to go on family walks and wants to stay at home this morning. Will he be able to persuade his parents that what he wants to do instead is worthwhile enough that they will grant his request? (*Do this in pairs or groups of three.*)

- Goldilocks has just been discovered by the three bears. They want her to explain why she's in their house. Goldilocks tries to think of all the excuses she can, but nothing seems to satisfy them. (*Do this in pairs or groups of four.*)

Leader in Role

- (*You play Goldilocks' mother.*) I am really worried about my daughter Goldilocks. She often wanders away from our house and gets into trouble. She doesn't seem to be afraid of anything, which is sometimes good, but I wish she would be a little more cautious. What can I do to help her realize that it can be dangerous to go off on your own? What ideas do you have for me?

Debate

- Half the class are the bears and their relatives, who want Goldilocks and her parents to take responsibility for her actions and the damages she caused. After all, she broke in the house, stole food, damaged furniture, and left a mess. The other half are Goldilocks' family, who claim she is just a curious child who enjoys finding new people to meet. They think the bears should be more tolerant. (*You may pretend to be a judge, but don't rule in favor of one side or the other. Imply that you have more important cases and you want them to come to some friendly agreement. Dismiss the case when both sides appear to feel satisfied with their compromises.*)

Related Activities

- The bear family writes an apologetic letter to Goldilocks for frightening her. Goldilocks also writes a letter of apology to the bears. What will each of the letters say? Write the letters in groups of three and read them aloud to the class.

- Create a newspaper appropriate for the bear community. Perhaps there might be articles or editorials about cases of breaking and entering or vandalism in the area; the food section might have recipes for porridge; classified ads might feature used furniture; or a "home" section might have an article on how to repair broken chairs. There might also be announcements of interesting events taking place on the weekend that bears would be attracted to and advertisements for products bears would like. What other interesting items might be covered?

- Baby bear is having a birthday. Plan his party for him, including the games to be played and the food to be served. (Remember what bears like to eat.) Baby Bear also wants to invite his friends and "the little girl who came here one day." Write an invitation to Goldilocks for him.

- Baby bear writes a letter to his grandparents, telling them all about the day a little girl came to his house. Write this letter the way you think baby bear would.

Three Billy Goats Gruff

Peter Christen Asbjørnsen

Summary: *Three goats from the Gruff family, who want to eat in a meadow on the other side of a bridge, must outwit a troll who threatens to eat them up.*

Selected Picture Books

Three Billy Goats Gruff. Retold by Paul Galdone. Houghton Mifflin/ Clarion, 1973. Galdone's drawings emphasize the folktale quality of the story.

The Three Billy Goats Gruff. Retold and illustrated by Janet Stevens. Harcourt, Brace, Jovanovich, 1987. This version has delightful pictures of the characters, including a little billy goat with a pacifier and a big billy goat with leather jacket and sunglasses.

Three Billy Goats Gruff. Illustrated by Marcia Brown. Harcourt, Brace, Jovanovich, 1957. Long a favorite, these illustrations clearly highlight the drama.

Solo Pantomime Activities

Pantomime Solo

- You are the troll asleep under the bridge. It's early in the morning and you didn't get much sleep last night. What will you look like waking up? As I count slowly to five, you wake up for the day.

- You're the big billy goat gruff, who's big and strong and not at all afraid of the mean old troll. Begin your walk across the bridge (*in place*).

- You're the troll, waiting under the bridge. It must be pretty boring just sitting there, waiting for someone to come by. Think of three things you might do to amuse yourself while you wait. I'll play some music (*"In the Hall of the Mountain King" from* Peer Gynt Suite *by Grieg*) and as I count to three, act out your three ideas. (*Children might decide to file their claws, floss their teeth, count blades of grass, or scare themselves by looking in the stream.*)

Narrative Pantomime

- You're the "great ugly Troll, with eyes as big as saucers and a nose as long as a poker." You gobble up everyone who crosses your bridge. Sniff, sniff, something tasty seems to be coming toward you. Better check it out. Peek up over the bridge and see what tasty morsel might be coming your way. Yum, yum, yum.

- You are the bridge, which has been walked on for many years. Show how you feel each step as people go over you. Here comes the little billy goat gruff—trip trap, trip trap; now the middle-sized one— TRIP TRAP, TRIP TRAP; and finally the big billy goat gruff— **TRIP TRAP, TRIP TRAP.** Goodness, let's hope that's all the traffic for today!

Solo Verbal Activities

Verbal Solo

- You're the littlest billy goat. Why did you go over the bridge? Didn't you know the troll was under there waiting for you? Weren't you taking a big chance? What made you think of the answer you gave to the troll?

- You're the big billy goat. How do you feel about having to protect your younger brothers all day long? Does it get a little tiresome? Do you really *want* to help them or do you feel you *have* to because of your size and age? What else do you do besides looking after them?

- You're the billy goat family. You have an interesting name—Gruff. Is that your real name or is that just what people call you? Do other goat families have this name? If so, do they spell it the same way as you do? (*You might pretend to be an interested census taker.*)

- You're the bridge. Tell us a little about your life. What's it like having the billy goats go over you? Do any other people or animals come by? Who built you? Are there any secrets you have to tell?

• You're the troll, practicing your questions and threats. How many different ways can you say the lines?

Paired and Group Pantomime Activities

Build a Place

• Apparently the troll lives under the bridge. Did you ever wonder what his home looks like? What sorts of things might he have under there? Create his living quarters and furnish them.

Mirroring

• In pairs, mirror the troll looking into the water, practicing his scary faces.

Frozen Picture

• In groups of four, organize a series of three frozen pictures, showing the fight between the troll and the big billy goat. Include the two younger billy goats as onlookers. The first picture might show the big billy goat meeting the troll; the second could show the billy goat ready to butt the troll; and the final picture might be of the billy goat triumphantly looking down at the troll in the water. Be sure to include the reactions of the younger billy goats.

Paired and Group Verbal Activities

Leader in Role

• (*You read a letter from the troll.*) "Dear Class, I have to go away for a few days and I'm worried about how I can guard my bridge. What could I do to make sure no one uses it while I'm gone? Leave your suggestions on the chalkboard and I will read them tonight. Thank you for helping me. (*signed*) The troll."

• (*You play the troll's mother or father confronting the billy goats. Be yourself, not mean and ugly, so as not to frighten the children or have them retaliate against you.*) I know you, you're the Gruff children. I want to talk to you. Why do you keep coming over my son's bridge? Can't you find another pasture to eat in instead of purposely antagonizing my child? How about planting your own garden and staying on your own side of the pasture?

- (*You play the troll's mother or father.*) Mr. and Mrs. Gruff, I have a complaint about your children. They are ruining my son's bridge every time they come past our house. The bridge is being damaged and my son is very upset about it. I'm sure you don't want this to continue any more than I do. What can we do to solve this problem?

- (*You play an interested neighbor or, for more authority, a pediatrician or school psychologist.*) Mr. and Mrs. Troll, I'd like to talk to you about your child. He seems to be very aggressive, always talking about gobbling people up. Why is he so angry? When did this behavior start? Is it possible something is troubling him? Perhaps this behavior is masking some other problems? (*After the discussion, thank them for their cooperation. If this seems to be an interesting discussion to the children, you might pick it up again at a later time with a letter from the teacher about the troll's latest behavior in school.*)

- (*You play the distraught mother of the troll.*) Doctor, I just don't know what to do about my child. He doesn't share his toys with other children; in fact, he fights with them constantly. I punish him and it doesn't seem to work. I'm at my wit's end and don't know what to do. Can you help me? (*Make a list together of the suggestions that are made. The guidance the children give should be plausible and nonviolent. If they give violent suggestions, tell them that you chose them as your doctor because you heard they were intelligent and gentle—and that's the kind of advice you want for your child. If children enjoy the activity, you can come back again on another day and ask for more advice on the troll's latest doings.*)

Debate

- (*Divide the class into trolls and billy goats.*) The Gruffs claim the pasture on the other side of the bridge is the best place to eat and goats should be allowed to go there. The trolls say they just want to live in peace and quiet under the bridge without being bothered by the sound of hooves all the time. What other points are made in this discussion? (*You might be the farmer who owns the field and just wants the goats and troll to get along.*)

Interview Panel

- (*Panel members all play the troll.*) Some questions that might be asked: What is it like sitting under a bridge all day waiting for your next meal to come by? When is the best time of day to catch someone? Do you ever let anyone else go by the way you did the littlest billy goat? Do you feel guilty after you have threatened or eaten someone? Do you really eat the billy goats, or do you just say that to scare them? What do your parents think of your behavior?

Improvised Scene

- The troll has just come home soaking wet from having fallen into the river. He tries to explain to his mother why he is wet—for the third time this week. He'd better leave out the part about getting into a fight with the billy goats. The scene is over when his mother gives him his punishment. Nothing physical (like spanking) is allowed!

Related Activities

- You are members of the traffic safety office. In groups, make up a list of rules for bridge use. Be sure to take care of the concerns of both the billy goats and the trolls. (*Compile the lists into one with the whole class.*)

- Study noise abatement rules such as those developed for communities near airports. Write a similar policy for bridge traffic, considering that home owners live under the bridge.

- Research various types of bridges and their construction. Design a new bridge for the troll and the billy goats that would solve everyone's problems.

- Search for other stories that have trolls in them. Compare the illustrations of the troll characters. Which do you like best?

- The story of the billy goats and the troll has become so popular the troll wants to capitalize on it. He now considers his bridge a tourist attraction and wants to get in the business of selling souvenirs. Design some appropriate souvenirs for him.

The Three Little Pigs

Joseph Jacobs

Summary: *Three pigs leave home to seek their fortune. The first builds a house of straw; the second, sticks; and the third, bricks. A wolf blows down the first two houses and eats the pigs. When he can't blow down the brick house, the wolf tries to trick the pig to come out of the house. But the third pig is too clever and outwits the wolf at his own game.*

Selected Picture Books

The Three Little Pigs. Illustrated by Erik Blegvad. Atheneum, 1984. Small pen-and-ink drawings colored in pencil show nice detail.

The Three Little Pigs. Written and illustrated by Gavin Bishop. Scholastic, 1990. This version has some appealing modern touches (the wolf has a Walkman and wears sunglasses).

The Three Little Pigs. Retold and illustrated by Jean Claverie. North-South, 1989. The pigs have a close relationship in this retelling and read about the big bad wolf's return in the *Forest Daily Mail*.

The Three Little Pigs. Written and illustrated by James Marshall Dial, 1989. A popular author and illustrator, Marshall has fun with his own little touches and cartoonlike illustrations.

The Three Little Pigs. Illustrated by William Pene du Bois. Viking, 1962. Charming pictures in a decidedly English setting.

The Three Little Pigs. Margot Zemach. Farrar, Straus and Giroux, 1988. The pigs in these watercolor illustrations have bristly faces and patched clothing.

Related Sources

The True Story of the Three Little Pigs! by A. Wolf. Written by Jon Scieszka
and illustrated by Lane Smith. Viking/Penguin, 1989. The wolf
claims he only wanted to borrow a cup of sugar and unfortunately
had a sneezing attack at the little pigs' door.

The Three Little Pigs and the Fox. Written by William H. Hooks and
illustrated by S. D. Schindler. Macmillan, 1989. An Appalachian
storyteller's version of the old tale, with a sister pig, Hamlet, who
tricks the fox.

"The Builders." Written by Sara Henderson Hay. From *Story Hour.* Doubleday, 1963. Also in *Reflections on a Gift of Watermelon Pickle,* edited
by Stephen Dunning, Edward Lueders, and Hugh Smith. Scott,
Foresman, 1966. The third little pig tells how he tried to warn his
brothers about their poor choices of homes.

"The Three Little Pigs." Written by Roald Dahl. From *Roald Dahl's Revolting Rhymes*. Knopf, 1983. The third little pig calls Red Riding Hood
to assist him. She kills the wolf (as she did in her story) and now has
two wolfskin coats—in addition to a pigskin traveling case!

Solo Pantomime Activities

Pantomime Solo

- First, show how a pig would build a house of straw. Next, show how
a pig would build a house of sticks. Finally, show how a pig would
build a house of bricks.

- What does the wolf do when he isn't chasing after little pigs? (*Discuss.*) Select three things you think he does and act them out as I
count from one to three. (*As an accompaniment to this activity, select
music that will fit any mood, since the wolf might do lighthearted activities
rather than frightful ones.*)

Narrative Pantomime

- You are one of the little pigs whose house has been blown down by
the wolf. Let's see how fast you can run (*in place*) to your brother's
house. Lock the door behind you, brace a wooden chair under the
doorknob, and close the curtains so the wolf can't peek in. Then hide
in the closet till your clever brother comes home from work. (*In some
versions of the story the first two pigs go to the third brother's house.*)

- When the third little pig saw the wolf at Shanklin Fair, he hid in a
butter churn. Let's see how a chubby little pig would have to struggle

to squeeze into a butter churn. Hurry, the wolf is getting closer! Don't forget to snap the lid on the top! Safe!

Solo Verbal Activities

Verbal Solo

- You are old Dame Pig, who is too poor to take care of her three little pigs any longer. How is it that you happened to get into this unfortunate financial state of affairs? What do you think will happen to your children? What particular worries do you have about them?

- You are one of the three pigs packing your little valise to leave home. What one favorite thing do you plan to take with you as you go off to seek your fortune? Tell us why it is so special to you.

- You're the wolf. You're so excited about your pork-chop dinner that you forget the little chant you always say each time you blow down a house. What other chant could you say instead?

- You are the wolf. Why are you so determined to eat this particular family of pigs? What did they ever do to you?

- You are the wolf heating up in the pot of water. Tell us some reasons why you shouldn't be cooked. Better hurry; the water is getting hotter by the second!

- You're one of the pigs. What is this little expression you and your brothers have—"not by the hair on my chinny-chin-chin"? What does that mean? Where did you learn it?

Storytelling

- You are the wolf and have just been frightened out of your wits by the great round thing (*the butter churn*) that came down the hill. You have run to the little pig's house and are telling him, as hurriedly as you can though you are out of breath, about the horrible beast that chased you. What story do you tell?

Paired and Group Pantomime Activities

Narrative Pantomime

- (*Divide the class into groups of three.*) You are three little pigs and have a huge cauldron filled with water. It's so heavy it takes all of you to carry it over to the fireplace. Walk ten steps, staying together, and hang the cauldron on the hook. Watch that you don't spill any water. Good!

Mirroring

- In pairs, be one of the little pigs shaving the hair on your chinny-chin-chin. Lather up well and use a straight razor very carefully. Watch that your snout doesn't get in the way.

Frozen Picture

- Show Dame Pig saying a tearful farewell to her three little ones.

- Show the wolf falling into the pot with a huge splash with the three little pigs watching.

- Show the wolf blowing down the straw house, then show him blowing down the stick house. How will these two pictures look different?

Paired and Group Verbal Activities

Conversation

- Dame Pig is having tea with her friends, who are talking about the accomplishments of their children. Dame Pig wants to brag about her three sons, too. But she'll have to leave out the part about the wolf getting the first two. What will she say instead? (*Divide the class into groups of three.*)

Interview

- The wolf has been huffing and puffing so much lately that he now has a sore throat. He goes to the doctor for help. The doctor examines him and asks questions to determine the cause. We'll compare doctors' notes afterward and then decide on our advice as a group and write out a prescription for him. (*Do this first in pairs and then as a whole group.*)

Debate

- The wolf has a bad reputation; a pig, a little girl with a red cloak, and a shepherd boy have made complaints. Three character witnesses (the wolf's former baby sitter, his scout leader, and a teacher) will speak in his behalf and answer questions from the citizens of the community, some of whom feel he should pay for his crimes, others of whom say he has good qualities that are being overlooked.

• In groups of five, create a television commercial for a building-supply company whose major clients are pigs thinking of buying homes. Some things to consider: What is your company's name? Do you have a slogan? What kinds of building supplies will you try to sell for wolfproof homes? What advertising techniques (e.g., testimonial, bandwagon, statistics) will you employ?

Leader in Role

• (*You play the wolf's mother.*) It's so nice to meet a nice group of wolves like yourselves—fine, upstanding young people. I just wish my son were more like you. He is so restless and seems to have no ambition. All he wants to do is go around the neighborhood threatening people who are littler and weaker than he is. I don't know what happened. Maybe he got in with the wrong crowd. I just don't know what to do. Since you know him, do you have any ideas about how to help him?

Improvised Scene

• The wolf's mother has sent him out to get a pig for dinner. But this time he comes home without one. What excuses will he give? How does his mother react? The scene ends when a decision is made about what they will eat tonight instead of pork.

Related Activities

• As the third little pig, write a letter to your mother telling her of your success. Tell about your brothers, too, but try not to worry her with their problems.

• Suppose the pig who built the straw house or the pig who built the stick house wanted to write a letter of complaint to the building supplier. What points would he make in his letter about the inferior materials? What will he propose be done?

• The three pigs decide to live together, but now the brick home has to be redesigned to accommodate all of them. Draw the floor plans of a house that would work well for three young pigs, each wanting his own privacy. Add a guest room for Dame Pig, who will be coming to visit them often.

• The three pigs decide to have a party to celebrate the capture of the wolf. What games might be played at the party that point out the wolf as the villain and the pigs as the heroes?

- The little pigs have their mother's famous and special recipe for wolf soup. Write it out, carefully explaining the little things that make it so special. What is the best way to serve it?

- The wolf has a cookbook featuring pork and ham dishes. Write out some of his favorite recipes. What other little cooking hints or clever sayings might be included?

- The wolf went to the doctor complaining of chest pains. The doctor discovers the wolf has been eating too much fat. Write out a week's diet that would be low on fat and cholesterol the doctor might give the wolf.

Little Red Riding Hood

Jakob & Wilhelm Grimm

Summary: *A little girl is sent to her grandma's house with a basket of treats. On the way she meets a wolf and tells him of her plans. He takes a shortcut to the grandma's house, eats her up, dresses in her bedclothes. Red Riding Hood arrives and is puzzled by her grandma's looks. She questions the wolf, who pops out of bed and eats her up also. A passing woodcutter cuts the wolf's stomach open and lets the girl and her grandmother out. (In the Perrault version, there is no rescue scene.)*

Selected Picture Books

Little Red Cap. Translated by Elizabeth D. Crawford and illustrated by Lisbeth Zwerger. Morrow, 1983. Earth tones dominate and lend the country flavor to the story.

Little Red Riding Hood. Retold and illustrated by Trina Schart Hyman. Holiday, 1983. In this Caldecott Honor book there are detailed drawings and borders and the most delightful little girl in high-top shoes.

Red Riding Hood. Retold and illustrated by James Marshall. Dial, 1987. Marshall's cartoonlike drawings keep the story lighthearted.

Related Sources

"The Grandmother." Written by Sara Henderson Hay. From *Story Hour*. Doubleday, 1963. Grandmother is lonely and may take in a stray mongrel.

Gunniwolf. Edited by Wilhelmina Harper and illustrated by William Wiesner. Dutton, 1967. A little girl escapes the wolf by singing sweetly. (See also: *Gunnywolf*. Written and illustrated by A. Delaney. Harper, 1988.)

"Little Red Riding Hood and the Wolf." Written by Roald Dahl. From *Roald Dahl's Revolting Rhymes*. Knopf, 1982. Little Red Riding Hood shoots the wolf with a pistol hidden in her knickers and is later seen wearing a wolfskin coat.

Lon Po Po. Translated and illustrated by Ed Young. Philomel, 1989. In this Red Riding Hood story from China, a woman leaves her three daughters at home alone while she visits their granny. A hungry wolf, disguised as the grandmother, attempts to get in the house but is thwarted. Caldecott Medal winner.

Solo Pantomime Activities

Narrative Pantomime

• You are the wolf hurriedly getting ready for Little Red Riding Hood's appearance. Get granny's nightgown on. You've never worn clothes like this before, so you'd better figure out quickly how to get it on. Watch out for the long sleeves; they can be tricky. There, looks pretty good. Oops, your tail's showing. Now get the sleeping cap on. Tuck in your ears. Take a quick look in the mirror. Hop in bed. Look tired and sick. Okay, here she comes! Freeze!

Transformation

• On the count of ten, you will slowly turn from the wily, wicked wolf into a poor, sickly grandmother.

Solo Verbal Activities

Verbal Solo

• You're Red Riding Hood's grandmother. We know you're very fond of your little granddaughter. Tell us, what is there about her that makes her so special?

• Grandmother, why do you live so far into the woods? Have you ever thought about getting a place closer to your relatives?

• You are Red Riding Hood's mother. Why did you send her on the visit to her grandmother's house? Surely you knew it was dangerous for her to go into the woods alone.

• You're the wolf. What do you do when you aren't stalking little girls in the woods or terrorizing grandmothers?

• You're a radio or television announcer reporting on the danger of wolves in the woods. What brief bulletin will you give for today's broadcast?

Paired and Group Pantomime Activities

Mirroring

• Little Red Riding Hood is checking out her new cape in the mirror. Try wearing it in different styles. Pose in different positions with it.

Count/Freeze Pantomime

• The woodcutter got a wolfskin to take home with him. Pantomime what he does with it.

Count/Freeze or Intragroup Pantomime

• Red Riding Hood loves her red cape so much that she wants everything in red. Act out things she has, uses, or wears that could be red.

Improvised Scene

• Play the scene in which the woodcutter hears the wolf snoring, slashes the wolf open, and saves grandmother and little girl. The scene ends when the grandmother and Red Riding Hood say goodbye to the woodcutter.

Paired and Group Verbal Activities

Sound Mime

• The woodcutter chopping a tree in the forest.

• The wolf snoring after his meal of grandmother and little girl.

• Red Riding Hood singing a little song as she picks flowers in the woods.

Improvised Scene

• Red Riding Hood is tired of taking trips through the forest to see her granny. What excuses will she give her mother today, and how will her mother entice her to go? The scene ends when Red Riding Hood takes the basket and goes out the door.

- (*Do this activity in pairs.*) The wolf is working with a voice coach on ways to disguise his voice to sound like a little girl and a grandmother. What hints and tips will the coach give? Is the wolf a good student? The scene ends when an appointment is made for the next lesson.

Interview and Leader in Role

- A police officer, patrolling the woods, stops the wolf for questioning. Where is he going? What is he planning to do? Are his answers acceptable? (*Do this activity in pairs and have the officers report to you, their chief.*)

- Grandmother is being visited by a social worker to see if other arrangements can be made for her care. Even if she recovers from her illness, she is still getting too old to live by herself. What seems to be the best solution? (*Have the students report their findings to you as Red Riding Hood's mother or father. Make a list of the solutions and compare them. Will any of them work from your point of view?*)

Debate

- Half the class represents the Society for the Protection of Wolves and Their Reputations. The other half represents Red Riding Hood and her relatives and neighbors. What arguments will be presented by both sides?

Related Activities

- Red Riding Hood needs instruction in what to do when meeting strangers in the woods and elsewhere. Make a list of dos and don'ts for her.

- Make a list of appropriate items, including food and other essentials, one might take to an elderly person who is not feeling well.

- Do research on wolves and find out what they really eat.

- Have older students act out the Dahl poem (*listed under "Related Sources"*) in groups of four, with one being "I."

The Gingerbread Boy

An American Tale

Summary: *Many tales around the world feature runaway food. In the American version of such stories, an old couple wish for a child. When the old woman bakes a gingerbread in the shape of a boy, it comes alive and runs away. Everyone chases the gingerbread boy. He is able to outrun them all—until he meets a sly fox.*

Selected Picture Books

The Gingerbread Boy. Written by Hilary Knight and illustrated by Scott Cook. Knopf, 1987.

The Gingerbread Boy. Written by David Cutts and illustrated by Joan E. Goodman. Troll, 1979.

The Gingerbread Boy. Illustrated by Paul Galdone. Houghton Mifflin/Clarion, 1975. Galdone's gleeful drawings convey the story's liveliness.

The Gingerbread Man. Written by Karen Schmidt. Scholastic, 1985. This is an easy-reader edition of the story.

Selected Variants

The Bun. Written by Marcia Brown. Harcourt, 1972. In this Russian version of the tale, a bun is made from the little bit of flour that can be scraped from the bottom of the bin.

The Funny Little Woman. Written by Arlene Mosel. Dutton, 1972. This story is based on the Japanese tale of a rolling rice ball that leads a woman into an underground world where she is held captive.

Journey Cake, Ho! Retold by Ruth Sawyer and illustrated by Robert McCloskey. Viking, 1953. This American Appalachian version of the gingerbread story is written by a noted storyteller and illustrated by an award-winning artist.

The Pancake. Written by Anita Lobel. Greenwillow, 1978. This story is based on the Swedish version.

Solo Pantomime Activities

Narrative Pantomime

- Be a ball of gingerbread dough. You're all curled up at first. As I count to ten, you will slowly unfold—as if being flattened with a rolling pin—and become the shape of a gingerbread child. First your left arm slowly takes shape, one . . . two . . . ; now your right arm, three . . . four. . . . Out rolls your left leg, five . . . six . . . ; then your right leg, seven . . . eight. . . . Last your head, nine . . . ten. Oh, what a handsome gingerbread child you are!

- You are the gingerbread boy. Peek out the oven door. Nobody's around! Open the door quietly and jump out. Begin running away (*in place*). Look back over your shoulder to see if anybody's chasing you. Yep, there they are. Tee, hee, hee. Jump over the gate and take off down the road lickety split! Whee! What fun! Whoa, now stop, sit down, and take a rest. Whew! Got away for now. Did you ever think life would be as exciting as this? Where do you think you might want to go and why? (*You might want them to answer this question while they're resting.*)

Count/Freeze Pantomime

- Pantomime a farm or a woodland animal that might have run after the gingerbread boy, and we'll guess which animal you are. Try to show what animal you are with your body and the way you move or eat rather than making the animal's sounds. (*Several children at a time can be the same animal or each may play a different animal.*)

- Be one of the animals or people who ran after the gingerbread boy. Show something you might have been doing when he ran by and laughed at you. What you choose to do and how you do it should help us identify who you are.

- Where would a gingerbread boy go if he could make a getaway and go off on his own? What would he like to do? Show us your idea of an adventure you think the gingerbread boy would like to have and we'll try to guess what it is.

• The people who chased the gingerbread boy wanted to eat him. When they didn't catch him, what did they eat instead? Pantomime a food they could eat, and we'll guess what it is.

Quieting Activity

• Be the fox who ate the gingerbread boy. You're nice and full and you take a good, long nap under a tree by the riverbank.

Solo Verbal Activities

Verbal Solo

• The gingerbread boy laughs as he runs. Let's hear the laugh a gingerbread cookie would have. (*Let three or four at a time try their laughs.*)

• Pretend you are the little old woman who has become famous for her gingerbread. You are appearing on a television cooking show. Explain your famous recipe and demonstrate how you make and bake a gingerbread cookie. This time, though, the finished cookie will not come alive.

• Pretend you are one of the animals or persons in the story that ran after the gingerbread boy. Tell us who you are and then give a reason why you think you should be the one—the only one—to get him.

Paired and Group Pantomime Activities

Improvised Scene

• Create the oven the gingerbread boy popped out of. When I give the signal, the gingerbread boy will open the oven door and jump out. (*This activity should be done in groups of five.*)

Mechanical Movement

• Suppose the little old woman had an electric mixer or food processer. Create either and show us how it works. (*Do this activity in groups of five.*)

Paired and Group Verbal Activities

Interview

- (*Do in pairs.*) The gingerbread boy interviews either the man or the woman to find out how they plan to take care of him/her. What does each party expect of the other?

Interview Panel

- (*The panel consists of gingerbread boys; the audience may pretend to be newspaper or television reporters.*) Questions that may be asked: At what point did you come alive in the oven—did it happen the moment you were first put in or later? What thoughts went through your little gingerbread head when you realized what was happening to you? At what point did you decide to run away? Why did you run away from home?

Leader in Role

- (*You play either the old man or the old woman.*) Good neighbors, thank you so much for coming to help us. I think if we all use our heads we can figure out a way to head off the little gingerbread boy, perhaps a kind of roadblock. The last we heard, he was headed toward the river. Would you get in groups of three and figure out a plan for us? Do you have any questions before you begin?

Interview and Leader in Role

- (*Do in pairs.*) One of you will be a neighbor of the old couple. You called the sheriff to report some strange things going on next door. The deputy comes and tries to find out some of the details. Take notes and I'll hear your report when your interview is ended. (*Afterward, you play the sheriff getting the deputies' reports.*)

- Two detectives are questioning the old couple, who have reported their child missing. What information can you find out? Is anything else missing? Do you suspect foul play? What clues can you find? What do the old couple think happened? (*Work in groups of four. Afterward, you play the chief of detectives.*)

Experts

- A panel of experts on the subject of runaway children appears on a television talk show. Relatives in the audience will have a chance to ask questions. What questions do the relatives ask and what advice do the experts give? (*You moderate as a talk show host.*)

Related Activities

- Write a different chant the gingerbread cookie might have said as he ran away from everyone.

- Draw a map of the path the gingerbread boy took as he ran away from everyone. Show the point at which he was caught.

- Research recipes for gingerbread cookies and select one to try.

- Draw a picture of a decorated gingerbread person. Besides icing, what other candy decorations could be put on and what would they represent?

- How many other stories about runaway food can you find?

- Suppose the gingerbread boy survived, grew up, and went to school. What subjects or lessons might a gingerbread child need to learn that are the same or different from ours? Make a schedule for a typical school day for a gingerbread child.

Hansel and Gretel

Jakob & Wilhelm Grimm

Summary: Two children are abandoned in the woods by their stepmother and weak-willed father because there is not food enough for them all. The children stumble upon a house made of cake and candy. The old woman who owns the house captures them and reveals herself as a witch. She forces Gretel to work for her and puts Hansel in a cage. Her intention is to eat them both, but Gretel cleverly outwits the witch and rescues her brother. They return home to discover the stepmother has died. The father is overjoyed to see them again, and with the riches the children have brought from the witch's house they live a happy life together.

Selected Picture Books

Hansel and Gretel. Translated by Elizabeth Crawford and illustrated by Lisbeth Zwerger. Morrow, 1979. This version has impressionistic drawings with strong images depicted in earth tones.

Hansel and Gretel. Retold by Ruth Belov Gross and illustrated by Winslow Pinney Pels. Scholastic, 1988. Detailed illustrations with depth and radiance intensify the story.

Hansel and Gretel. Illustrated by Susan Jeffers. Dial, 1980. Detailed drawings show a grandmotherly-looking witch.

Hansel and Gretel. Retold by Rika Lesser and illustrated by Paul O. Zelinsky. Dodd, Mead, 1984.

Hansel and Gretel. Retold and illustrated by James Marshall. Dial, 1990. A simple retelling of the tale with some bits of humor and a witch who bears a striking resemblance to Viola Swamp from *Miss Nelson Is Missing* by the same author.

Hansel and Gretel. Translated by Eleanor Quarrie and illustrated by
    Anthony Browne. Franklin Watts, 1982. This version presents a
    contemporary setting, illustrating urban life and poverty. The illus-
    trations suggest that the witch and the stepmother are one.

Related Sources

"The Lost Ones" and "Juvenile Court." Written by Sara Henderson Hay.
    From *Story Hour*. Doubleday, 1963. The first poem describes the
    children forsaken in the woods; in the second, police question their
    killing of the witch.

Solo Pantomime Activities

Narrative Pantomime and Pantomime Solo

• You are Hansel or Gretel trying to find your way out of the woods.
  You're very hungry because you haven't had anything to eat for three
  days. Suddenly you notice a pretty little bird, and you stop to listen
  to his sweet song. He flies off and you follow. Now he perches on the
  roof of a little house. You go closer and discover the house is made
  of gingerbread, cakes, and candy. You can hardly believe your eyes!
  Break off just a little to taste. It's so good you begin taking handfuls
  to satisfy your hunger. Ahhh, at last, food!

• You're the witch. Even though you cannot see very far, you have a
  keen sense of smell and you know when humans are coming close to
  your house. What might you be doing when you get the first whiff
  of Hansel and Gretel approaching your cottage? What one important
  thing will you do next? Freeze when you get to your front door and
  are ready to open it. Hold your frozen position until everyone is
  finished. (*They will probably not all freeze at the same time. Afterward,
  ask the children what their "important thing" was.*)

• Poor Hansel, in his cage, was given the best food to eat while Gretel
  was given nothing but crayfish shells. Pretend you are Hansel or
  Gretel eating. By the way you eat your food, I'll know who you are.

• While Hansel is in a cage and being fattened up, Gretel has to work
  around the house. Think of three chores the witch makes you do. As
  I count one, two, three, act out each of these three chores.

• You are the witch and you've been waiting four weeks for Hansel to
  get fat. But he seems to be as skinny as ever. Today you've decided to

go ahead and eat him anyway. You're in your kitchen baking bread to go with your meal. But remember you cannot see very well and you have to go about the kitchen on your crutch. You hurry as fast as you can because you're so hungry for a tasty boy. While I play the music, let's see you at work. (*Suggestion: Use Saint-Saens' "Danse Macabre," played at fast speed, for this exercise.*)

Quieting Activity

• You are Hansel or Gretel, tired and weary from your wandering through the forest. You lie down to sleep for the night. (*Play "Prayer" from Humperdinck's opera* Hansel and Gretel *underneath this exercise.*)

Solo Verbal Activities

Verbal Solo

• You are the witch. Why didn't you call the police when you discovered the children eating your house? Have there been other trespassers on your property? What did you do to them?

• You're Hansel and Gretel's schoolteacher. From what you've seen, what sort of children are they? What are they like as students? What are their favorite subjects? What do you and their parents talk about at your parent-teacher conferences? Do you have any predictions for their future?

Paired and Group Pantomime Activities

Narrative Pantomime

• Hansel and Gretel try to find their way through the forest. It is tangled and thick with undergrowth and difficult to pass through. The branches seem to reach out toward them menacingly. Some of you will be the trees and others will be Hansel and Gretel. No touching is allowed. Show how it might have looked as the two children were trying to make their way through the woods. (*Half the class can be trees at their desks. Line up the rest of the children in pairs and let them go around the room and past the trees. For an even more dramatic effect, turn the lights down and play mysterious music.*)

Build a Place

• Create the witch's house. You're special construction workers who've been called in to do this delicate job. You probably won't be able to use regular tools. How might you put the house together and what different types of cakes, cookies, and candies might be used?

Frozen Picture

- (*Do in groups of six, seven, or eight.*) Create two frozen pictures of the witch's house. The first picture will show the house the way Hansel and Gretel found it, and the second picture will show the way the house looked after they nibbled at it.

Improvised Scene

- The witch kindly invites Hansel and Gretel into her house. She serves them milk and pancakes with sugar, apples, and nuts. Hansel and Gretel are so hungry they do not notice anything strange about her behavior, but when they are not looking, she eyes them hungrily. Let's see some of this scene, which will end when Hansel and Gretel finish eating.

- (*Do in groups of six.*) Create the witch's oven complete with an oven door. I'll come around and check to see how it opens. I wonder if I'll find anything in the oven?

Paired and Group Verbal Activities

Storytelling Through Sound

- Work out the sounds that would be needed to tell the story in outline form. Suggested scenes are Hansel and Gretel lost in the woods; the discovery of the witch's candy house; the sudden appearance of the witch; the imprisonment of Hansel and Gretel; Gretel's triumph over the witch; and Hansel and Gretel's joyous reunion with their father.

Debate

- Hansel and Gretel's father and stepmother are arguing about the lack of food and how they will feed themselves and the children. The stepmother wants to abandon the children in the woods, while the father tries to argue for other ways to solve the problem. What reasons will each give for his or her point of view?

- (*Do in groups of four.*) Two friends of Hansel and Gretel's come to play with them. The parents make excuses for Hansel and Gretel's absence, but something doesn't sound right about their story. What questions will the children ask? How will the parents try to convince the friends that everything is fine?

- Relatives are debating whether Hansel and Gretel should return to their family or go to a foster home. Which solution seems best? Are any other alternatives suggested?

- The townspeople debate whether Hansel and Gretel are really telling the truth about a witch, a cake and candy house, and their story of murder in self-defense. And what about all the jewels they returned with? Half feel there must be more to the story; the other half believe in the children's innocence.

Improvised Scene

- A helpful neighbor who lives some distance away has noticed more activity than usual in and around the elderly woman's house. When the neighbor pays a call and asks questions, the old woman seems friendly enough, but doesn't seem to want to reveal any information. What questions does the neighbor ask and what excuses will the witch give? (*You might brainstorm a list of possible questions beforehand. This activity could also be played as leader in role, with you being the neighbor and all the children being the witch.*)

- A door-to-door salesperson has heard that a lot of cooking goes on in this house in the woods and tries to sell the old woman some kitchen utensils. There's even a special on this week. The witch is interested, but is very busy with her bread baking and the special meal she is planning. How long can the salesperson hold her attention with the clever gadgets and the good prices? (*If you use props for the gadgets you'll be adding the Imagination Game to the activity.*)

Interview Panel

- (*Set up a panel made up of Hansel, Gretel, and the father, two persons playing each role.*) Now that the family has the jewels, they have become rich and famous. They are being interviewed by magazine reporters about how their life is different from the way it was before.

Experts

- The panel of experts are builders of gingerbread houses.

Conversation

- A group of neighbors are discussing why they haven't seen Hansel and Gretel for some time; the children in the group have noticed their absence from school. What would this discussion sound like? What kinds of information and questions would come out in the conversation?

Related Activities

- Create a recipe book the witch might have used.

- Write an advertisement for the witch's house for the real estate section of the newspaper. What good features will you want to point up and what questionable features will you have to downplay?

- After the witch's death, a diary is discovered in her house. What are some of the entries in it?

- Write an obituary for the witch; write another for the stepmother.

- Make a model of a gingerbread house. Many recipes, both simple and elaborate, can be found in magazines at holiday time. As an added activity, consider ways to make miniature furniture from cake, cookies, and candy. As an alternative, a cardboard model could be constructed.

Cinderella

CHARLES PERRAULT

Summary: *This popular tale is over a thousand years old and has hundreds of variants around the world. Cinderella, so called because she often sits in the chimney corner among the cinders, is mistreated by her stepmother and stepsisters. With the aid of a fairy godmother who outfits her in grand elegance, she meets and marries the prince. Through it all, Cinderella is as assertive as she is lovely, overcoming the barriers her stepfamily sets before her and eventually gaining what is her due.*

Selected Picture Books

Cinderella; or The Glass Slipper. Translated from Charles Perrault and illustrated by Marcia Brown. Scribner's, 1954. The Caldecott-Award-winning drawings are done in a combination of ink line, paint, and chalk in pastel shades.

Cinderella. Retold by Amy Ehrlich and illustrated by Susan Jeffers. Dial, 1985. The exquisite detail of the jacket illustration makes for a very realistic-looking Cinderella.

Cinderella. Retold and illustrated by Paul Galdone. McGraw-Hill, 1978. This illustrator's drawings are lively and strong and less romantic.

Cinderella. Illustrated by Nonny Hogrogian. Greenwillow, 1981. A magical hazel tree and a fairy dove replace the godmother in this softly illustrated Grimm version of the tale.

Cinderella. Retold by Barbara Karlin and illustrated by James Marshall. Little, Brown, 1989. Marshall's cartoonlike drawings tell the story tongue in cheek. The fairy godmother joins the family in the castle at the end.

Selected Variants

"Ashpet." Collected by Richard Chase in *Grandfather Tales*. Houghton Mifflin, 1948. This is an American Applachian version in which Cinderella attends a barn dance.

The Egyptian Cinderella. Written by Shirley Climo and illustrated by Ruth Heller. Crowell, 1989. An Egyptian slave from Greece, Rhodopis, becomes queen to Pharaoh Amasis (570–526 B.C.). This is one of the world's oldest versions of the tale, based on both fantasy and fact.

Princess Furball. Written by Charlotte Huck and illustrated by Anita Lobel. Morrow, 1989. This version in picture book format is similar to the English tale "Catskin," and the Grimm brothers' "Many Furs" or "Thousand Furs."

Tattercoats. Retold by F. S. Steel and illustrated by D. Goode. Bradbury, 1976. Joseph Jacobs originally recorded this English version of an old tale.

Yeh-Shen. Retold by Ai-Ling Louie and illustrated by Ed Young. Philomel, 1982. In this Chinese version of the story, a fish takes the place of the fairy godmother.

Related Sources

"Cinderella." Written by Roald Dahl. From *Roald Dahl's Revolting Rhymes*. Knopf, 1983. This is a gory version that includes the chopping off of heads.

"Interview." Written by Sara Henderson Hay. From *Story Hour*. Double-day, 1963. Cinderella's mother speaks to the press, telling how her stepdaughter spread lies about the family after being named Miss Glass Slipper of the Year.

The Paper Bag Princess. Written by Robert Munsch. Annick, 1980. This is a turnabout tale of a young princess who cleverly rescues a young prince from a dragon. She rejects him after he proves to be an un-grateful snob.

Petronella. Written by Jay Williams. Parents Magazine Press, 1973. (See also: "Petronella." Written by Jay Williams. In *A Storybook from Tomi Ungerer*. Tomi Ungerer, ed. Franklin Watts, 1974.) In this reversal tale the heroine rescues a prince who's not worth the effort; in fact, his alleged kidnapper turns out to be far more interesting.

Prince Cinders. Written by Babette Cole. Putnam, 1988. A fairy gives a small, skinny prince a new look and the chance to go to the Palace Disco. Older students will appreciate this one.

Solo Pantomime Activities

Pantomime Solo

• Be Cinderella, dressed in rags, sitting in the chimney corner among cinders. Your stepsisters have gone off to the ball, and you are left alone feeling wretched. How will your body and face show how you are feeling? (*Whisper*)When I say, It's magic! pretend your fairy godmother touches you with her wand, and you are dressed for the ball in the loveliest ball gown imaginable! How will your body and face show what you are feeling now? (*Cue*) (*Afterward discuss what thoughts were going through their [Cinderella's] heads in each instance.*)

• Where do you suppose Cinderella's fairy godmother might have come from and what might she have been doing before her sudden appearance? (*Discuss briefly.*) Now, you are Cinderella's fairy god-mother. Think of three things you might be doing when you "get the message" that Cinderella is in need of help. As I count to three, act out each one of your three ideas.

Slow- and Fast-Motion Pantomime

• While Cinderella works all day cooking, cleaning, and scrubbing, her stepsisters live a life of luxury. As I play the fast music, you will be Cinderella doing your many chores; when the slow music plays, you will be one of the stepsisters living a life very different from that of Cinderella. (*Switch back and forth between fast and slow music a couple of times. Use either two different musical selections or change speeds for the same selection. Consider Serge Prokofiev's "Cinderella."*)

• Cinderella is afraid her stepmother and stepsisters will find the one slipper she has left so she plans to hide it. Pretend that you're Cin-derella, looking for the best hiding place you can find, but it takes you three tries before you settle on what you consider the perfect spot. As the music plays and I count to three, hide your slipper. (*Afterward you may become Cinderella's best friend and whisper to her about whether she succeeded and if she might like to share her secret with you.*)

Solo Verbal Activities

Verbal Solo

• (*The students are Cinderella's father; you can pretend to be an interested bystander or perhaps a neighbor and ask some of the following questions.*) We understand, sir, you've recently remarried. From what you can tell, how is your daughter getting along with her new stepmother and stepsisters? What evidence do you have to support those statements? It must be very difficult not to show favoritism in your situation; how do you manage that? I noticed that your daughter seems to be wearing plainer clothes these days, rather more casual than your new wife and her daughters. Is there some reason for this?

• You are Cinderella wishing you could go to the ball, when your godmother appears and asks what is the matter. Explain to her why you're so unhappy. What will you say to persuade her to help you? (*You can respond as the godmother, though you shouldn't be too quick to grant Cinderella's wish. Perhaps this is a bigger task than you've ever done before and you're not sure you can handle it.*)

• The fairy godmother sends Cinderella to the garden to get a pumpkin. Suppose Cinderella can only find an eggplant [cucumber, cabbage, radish]. What would you, as the fairy godmother, turn it into? Let's hear the magic spell you would use. (*You could respond as Cinderella or as someone who's particularly interested in magic. See also the followup activity under "Improvised Scene."*)

Paired and Group Pantomime Activities

Mirroring

• (*Do in pairs.*) The stepsisters have full-length mirrors so they can see themselves from head to toe. Be one of the stepsisters giving yourself a final lookover in preparation for the ball. Let us see what you are wearing by the way you adjust everything and attend to the little details.

• Now let's show (*in groups of eight*) the two stepsisters getting ready for the ball, assisted by the stepmother and Cinderella, all mirrored.

Transformation

• (*Do in groups of eight.*) Form the famous pumpkin. On the count of ten, slowly change into Cinderella's beautiful, gilded coach.

Build a Place

• Create the kitchen Cinderella worked in most of the day.

• Create the stepsisters' room [or the prince's quarters in the palace] as a contrast to the kitchen.

• Create a room suited to the fairy godmother. Think about the kinds of furnishings a fairy godmother's house would have and items she might need in her line of work. Consider also what her life might be like when she isn't going around doing magic for other people.

Count/Freeze Pantomime

- Perform one of Cinderella's chores for us to guess.

- You're a person who has been invited to the prince's ball. Put on an article of clothing or beautify yourself in some way to get yourself ready for such a grand occasion. We'll guess what you're doing and perhaps even what kind of person you might be.

Frozen Picture

- (*Do in groups of three.*) Show the stepmother and stepsisters all ready for the ball; next, show how they look when the prince enters the ballroom; finally, show how they look when the prince dances all night with Cinderella and pays no attention to them.

- (*Do in groups of eight.*) Show the scene at the ball when Cinderella dashes out at midnight. What different reactions might the guests have?

- (*Do in groups of five.*) Create the scene of the stepsisters trying on the glass slipper.

Paired and Group Verbal Activities

Interview Panel

- (*Set up a panel of fairy godmothers.*) Questions that might be asked: What is a godmother? Where do you come from? How did you get to be Cinderella's fairy godmother? How did you know she needed your help? Are you a godmother to anyone else? Does everyone have a godmother? Where does your magic come from? Why did the spell last only until midnight? What other tricks can you perform?

- (*Set up a panel of mice, lizards, or rats; let the children choose the animal they wish to be.*) Questions that might be asked: What did you think of the ball? What did you do while Cinderella was inside the palace? What was it like for those of you who were turned into humans? Did the fact that you were really an animal underneath cause difficulties for you? Do you have any souvenirs of your experience? Are you happier as you are now, or would you like to stay in the other form? (*The audience may be the animals' family members questioning them after their return.*)

• (*Set up a panel of various townspeople and/or residents of the palace; you may wish to let the children create more specific roles for themselves.*) Questions that might be asked: What were your impressions of the ball? Describe the music, decorations, and food. Did you see the mysterious princess? What did you think of her? Who were some of the people you met? If you were able to recall only one thing about the event years from now, what would you want that one remembrance to be? (*The audience may be society reporters for the newspaper.*)

Debate

• The king wants to give a ball so the prince can meet the eligible young women of the kingdom. The queen thinks balls are too expensive and argues for a cheaper party, perhaps a garden tea. We already know who wins this debate; what we want to know is how the king was able to convince the queen to his point of view.

• One of the mice doesn't want to be turned into a horse. What are his reasons? The fairy godmother uses persuasion, not magic, to get him to cooperate. Will he be convinced when time is called?

• Now that the rat has been turned into a coachman and has a chance to see what life is like out in the world of humans, he doesn't want to return to being a rat. The fairy godmother isn't sure a permanent change would be for the best. After each gives his or her opinions, what final decision do they reach?

Conversation

• The stepsisters are trying on everything in their wardrobes but still can't decide what they will wear to the ball. Their nerves are on edge, and they argue over the most trivial things. Let's hear a little of this unpleasantness. (*Ring a small bell to begin and end these shared conversations.*)

• (*Divide the class into a number of small groups.*) You are guests at the ball. When I call your group's number, let us hear your party-type conversation with each other.

Improvised Scene

• (*Divide the class into groups of three.*) Cinderella greets her stepsisters when they return from the ball and pretends she has been asleep while they were gone. They answer her questions about what happened, without realizing she is the mysterious princess. She hides her delight at their story. The scene ends when the stepmother (*you as leader*) says it is time for bed.

- How would the story change if instead of turning a pumpkin into a coach, the fairy godmother had turned an eggplant into a motorcycle [a carrot into a spaceship; a radish into a hot-air balloon]? Enact the story from this moment to the end. (*Do in groups of five.*)

- Glass slippers are now all the rage. In groups of three, create a television commercial for glass slippers of all sizes and shapes. (*Each group should demonstrate one of the persuasive strategies used by advertisers: the bandwagon approach, the testimonial, research, and so on.*)

- Cinderella is now living in the palace but continues to rely on her fairy godmother for help with her royal work. How can the fairy godmother help Cinderella see that she can solve her own problems? (*Do this exercise in pairs, or in groups of three to include the prince.*)

- (*Divide the class into groups of five.*) Create an improvisation that shows who the fairy godmother goes on to help now that Cinderella doesn't need her any more.

Leader in Role

- (*Pretend to be someone wanting a fairy godmother.*) Cinderella's fairy godmother really did a lot of nice things for her. I wonder how a person gets a fairy godmother? Can you help me get one? (*You try the suggestions the children give you [crying, saying magical words, waving a magic wand] but nothing works. If someone suggests advertising for one, you might write an appropriate ad together. Sometimes children offer to be your fairy godmother; this might be followed up with interviews for those who wish to apply for the job. Children might be paired with each other for these interviews.*) Discussion questions: What purpose does a fairy godmother serve? How necessary is a fairy godmother? What else might one do if fairy godmothers seem to be in short supply?

- (*You are Cinderella's stepmother.*) I have a problem to discuss with you, and I think you are the only ones who can help me. You see, I have a stepdaughter who has a tendency to make up stories about her family. The rumors have spread far and wide and put us all in a bad light—for years. What has she told you about me or her stepsisters? (*Try to explain away the various points the children present.*) I do housework, too. We all have to pitch in. No one *forced* Cinderella to sit in those ashes. She could have gone to the ball but told *me* she was too tired to go. (*You might also give a reason to leave the group—I have guests coming to tea today—and let them continue the discussion on their own. You return later as yourself to find out their conclusion about the stepmother.*) Discussion questions: Who is telling the truth? Are things always as they seem?

• (*You are a royal messenger.*) I have a letter for you from Cinderella. It reads: "Dear Friends, Now that I am a princess I feel my nickname Cinderella is really inappropriate. What new name could you suggest for me that would reflect the royal position I now hold? Thank you for any help you can give me. Ever in your debt, Her Royal Highness, the Princess, a.k.a. Cinderella."

Related Activities

• Write the prince's invitation to the ball. What does it say? How does it look?

• The prince orders the glass slippers to be placed on display in the royal museum. Write a description/explanation of the sort that accompanies such historic items.

• Write out and deliver the messenger's proclamation about finding the mysterious, lost princess.

• The stepsisters write a letter of apology to Cinderella, asking for her forgiveness for the way they treated her. Write Cinderella's reply.

• Cinderella writes in her diary about how her life has changed. Will she write about any changes she feels in herself? If she is the same Cinderella she was before, how is she coping with her new life?

• How many variants of the Cinderella story can the students find? Make a list of the differences noted in each one.

Jack and the Beanstalk

JOSEPH JACOBS

Summary: *Jack trades the family cow for so-called magical beans. When they grow into a huge beanstalk, Jack climbs it and finds a giant's castle at the top. While the giant sleeps, Jack takes the giant's bags of gold, a hen that lays golden eggs, and a singing harp. As Jack climbs down the beanstalk, the giant chases him. When Jack reaches the bottom, he hurriedly chops down the beanstalk, kills the giant, and enjoys the wealth with his mother.*

Selected Picture Books

Jack and the Beanstalk. Retold and illustrated by Lorinda Bryan Cauley. Putnam, 1983. Full-color oil paintings featuring ruddy-faced characters resembling wood carvings and a huge giant with a spiked arm band characterize this version.

Jack and the Beanstalk. Retold and illustrated by John Howe. Little, Brown, 1989. Stunning, full-color paintings tell the story with vigor.

Jack and the Beanstalk. Retold and illustrated by Steven Kellogg. Morrow, 1991. A highly popular author and illustrator lends his particular style to the traditional story.

Jack and the Beanstalk. Retold by Susan Pearson and illustrated by James Warhola. Simon & Schuster, 1989. This is another fine rendition of the story.

Related Sources

"Jack and the Beanstalk." Written by Roald Dahl. From *Roald Dahl's Revolting Rhymes*. Knopf, 1983. The giant smells an Englishman because Jack needs a bath!

Jack the Giant Killer. Written by Beatrice Schenk de Regniers and illustrated by Anne Wilsdorf. Atheneum, 1987. This lively retelling in contemporary poetry is accompanied with cartoonlike illustrations.

Jack and the Wonder Beans. Written by James Still and illustrated by Margot Tomes. Putnam, 1977. This Appalachian storyteller's version of the tale is complete with local color and language. Another Appalachian version is *Jack and the Bean Tree*. Written and illustrated by Gail E. Haley. Crown, 1986.

Jim and the Beanstalk. Written by Raymond Briggs. Addison-Wesley, 1970. In this modernized retelling, the giant is getting old and asks Jim to get him some eyeglasses, dentures, and a red wig.

"Story Hour." Written by Sara Henderson Hay. From *Story Hour*. Doubleday, 1963. The poet asks if anyone is sorry for the giant Jack murdered.

Solo Pantomime Activities

Pantomime Solo

• You are Jack in the giant's castle. His wife has just told you to hide. As I count to three, show three different places you try to hide in. The first two you don't like for some reason; the third will be the best spot. You'll stay there until I tell you it's safe to come out.

• You are Jack in the giant's castle. The giant's wife is used to cooking huge meals for the giant, so she gives you an enormous plate of food to eat. How will you manage the giant-sized food and eating utensils set before you? I'll see if I can tell what you're eating by the way you handle it.

Fast-Motion Pantomime

• You are Jack, climbing down the beanstalk for the last time, with the giant close behind you. When you get to the bottom you have trouble finding the axe to chop down the beanstalk. You finally locate it and chop down the beanstalk in the nick of time. As I play the music, you will do all this in fast motion.

Narrative Pantomime

• You are the hen that lays golden eggs. You are laying your first egg. Get yourself comfortably settled on your nest. You lay an egg and get up to look at it. It's golden! You're very excited! You must be very special! How do you react (*silently*) to this discovery of yours? Sit back down on your nest and rest. You'll need all your strength to be such an important hen.

Solo Verbal Activities

Verbal Solo

- You are the hen that lays golden eggs. You've just laid your first one. Let's hear your special cackle to announce your achievement. Who will you tell about the egg? What do you plan to do with it? What special methods will you devise to protect it?

- You are the singing harp, and you can talk. Consider what your voice might sound like, and then tell us in that voice about yourself. Where did you come from? How did you get to be such a special harp? Are there other singing harps in your family? What do you think of the giant who now has you in his possession? What kind of master is he? What secrets can you can tell us?

- You are Jack's mother. What do you think of Jack's trade, now that there is a huge beanstalk outside your window? Do you still think the beans are worthless?

Sound Effects

- When the giant snores, the whole house shakes. Now, there are various ways people snore; each style is unique. What will your snore be like? (*Check some volunteers.*) We'll try a quiet snore first. (*Raise sound indicator as desired; students will have to keep one eye open to watch.*)

- The snore that shakes the whole house also shakes the giant. Let's see that snore rather than hear it. You'll still have to watch the sound indicator, but this time it will show the *intensity* of your snore—not the volume.

Imagination Game

- Show some props to the students and ask what uses the giant may have for them. They will have to keep in mind the size of the props in relation to the giant: his uses for the objects would probably be different from ours.

Paired and Group Pantomime Activities

Frozen Picture

- (*Do in groups of five.*) Create the scene we see after the giant has fallen from the chopped beanstalk. Who are the others in the picture?

Build a Place

- Create the cottage Jack and his mother live in. You'll be taking out the old furnishings and bringing in new items they purchased after they become wealthy.

Narrative Pantomime

- With two people at the head and two at the feet, pretend to carry the dead giant out of town. The pairs should remain about six feet apart at all times and treat the "body" with respect. (*Sidecoach students to walk up hill, cross a stream on stepping stones, go faster or slower, and so on.*)

Paired and Group Verbal Activities

Sound Mime

- Jack cutting down the beanstalk with an axe.

- The giant's wife kneading bread dough made of human bones.

- The giant eating a huge feast—everything from soup to nuts.

- The giant sniffing the blood of an Englishman as he tries to find someone in his castle.

- The giant counting his gold coins, then going to sleep snoring.

- The harp playing and singing a lullaby.

Leader in Role

- (*You play the giant's wife.*) Now that the giant, my home, and even the beanstalk are gone, I have no place to go. I'd like to get a job and make some money so I can support myself. But what kind of job could I get? Can you help me think of some jobs I might be suited for? Being a giant's wife ought to qualify me for something interesting, don't you think?

- (*You play the town mayor.*) Council members, Jack has discovered that there is one bean left and he has brought it to me. However, it doesn't look the same as the others that produced the beanstalk. We must decide what should be done with it. I'd like you to work in groups and make a list of the various things that might be done with the bean and any consequences of those actions. I have some paperwork to catch up on and shall return in a short while to hear your ideas.

Interview

- (*Set up a panel of giant's wives.*) Questions that might be asked: Why did you help Jack hide from the giant? How did you and the giant meet each other? What was your life like married to him? What happened to you after the beanstalk was chopped down and the giant was killed?

- (*Set up a panel of strangers.*) Questions that might be asked: Where did the beans come from? How did you know Jack's name? What did you want with a cow that doesn't give milk? Why didn't you plant the beans yourself? Did you ever visit Jack and his mother again? Did you know Jack would find the giant's castle?

- (*Set up a panel of giants.*) Questions that might be asked: Where did you get the gold, the singing harp, and the hen that lays the golden eggs? How did your castle get up in the sky? Is there any other way to reach the castle besides climbing a beanstalk? Why do you eat little boys? What about little girls?

Debate

- Half the class will be the citizens of the town, registering their complaints about the huge, unsightly beanstalk and demanding that the city officials do something about its removal. The other half of the class will be the officials trying to explain why there is no simple answer to the problem. What decision will be reached? (*You might moderate as the mayor, who is neutral and yet tries to please both sides.*)

- The giant's wife, her fatherless child, and a castle servant claim Jack should be punished for murdering the giant. Three people—Jack's mother, the man with the beans, and the singing harp—will speak on Jack's behalf. The class may ask questions and decide if there is enough evidence to put Jack on trial. (*If students decide on a trial, you may wish to carry that out also.*)

Improvised Scene

- Neighbors of Jack and his mother look out the window one morning and notice the giant beanstalk. Who are the neighbors and what will their conversation sound like? (*This activity works well for groups of four.*)

- The hen that lays the golden eggs tells another hen about it. The friend finds it hard to believe. What will their conversation sound like—in hen talk? (*Students try this out simultaneously; those who want to share their experience may do so.*)

• The giant's wife tries to convince her husband that he does not smell the blood of an Englishman. What will she tell him it is? How does he respond?

• Jack has to convince the giant's wife to let him in the castle and feed him. The wife hesitates because of what has happened in the past to other boys. What does Jack say that convinces her to let him in?

Related Activities

• Instead of fee fi fo fum, come up with a new chant for the giant—perhaps one that's less violent or that makes us like him and feel sorry for him. Chant it for us.

• Plant some bean seeds and study their growth.

• Make out a grocery list for the giant and his wife for one week. Plan dinner menus for each night.

• One of Jack's neighbors writes a letter detailing the damage caused to his house when the giant fell on it. The neighbor thinks Jack should be responsible for the damages. Jack hires a lawyer to write a response. What will the letter say?

Rumpelstiltskin

JAKOB & WILHELM GRIMM

Summary: *A miller tells the king that his daughter can spin straw into gold. With the aid of a little man, who makes her promise to give her firstborn to him, the miller's daughter does, indeed, spin straw into gold. The king happily marries her. The little man returns to the queen to claim his reward. She pleads not to have to give up her baby, so he makes a second bargain, saying she may keep the child if she can guess his name. When she surprises him by discovering his name, he disappears in a rage and is never heard from again.*

Selected Picture Books

Rumpelstiltskin. Retold and illustrated by Donna Diamond. Holiday, 1983. Detailed pencil drawings create the illusion of black-and-white photographs.

Rumpelstiltskin. Retold and illustrated by Paul Galdone. Houghton Mifflin/Clarion, 1985. The full-color watercolor wash drawings reflect the folk quality of the story.

Rumpelstiltskin. Retold by Alison Sage and illustrated by Gennady Spirin. Dial, 1991. The detailed illustrations in this version are reminiscent of the work of Renaissance painters.

Rumpelstiltskin. Written by Edith H. Tarcov and illustrated by Edward Gorey. Scholastic, 1973. Black line drawings in the artist's easily recognizable style enhance the story's old-world setting.

Rumpelstiltskin. Retold and illustrated by Paul O. Zelinsky. Dutton, 1986. The beautiful illustrations in this edition received a Caldecott Honor Award.

Selected Variants

Tom Tit Tot. Written by Joseph Jacobs. Retold and illustrated by Evaline Ness. Scribner's, 1965. A young woman's mother tells the king she can spin five skeins in a day, whereupon he marries her. She makes a pact with a little devil to do the spinning, but in guessing his name she is saved.

Duffy and the Devil. Retold by Harve Zemach and illustrated by Margot Zemach. Farrar, Straus and Giroux, 1973. A lazy maid makes a bargain with the devil to spin and knit. Her employer, an old squire, is so pleased with the work, he marries her. The old housekeeper helps Duffy discover the devil's name, but the squire loses his clothes in the process.

Solo Pantomime Activities

Pantomime Solo

- You are one of the king's servants and are carrying bales of straw into a large room and piling them up. The bales are heavy, but you must handle them carefully and not lose any pieces, as they will soon be turned into gold. As I count to five, stack five bales.

- You are Rumpelstiltskin. You are convinced the queen will never guess your name and you'll therefore get her baby. As I play the music, do the little dance you always do when you are excited. (*Any spritely music will do.*)

- You are Rumpelstiltskin, enraged and furious after the queen guesses your name. As I count to ten, you will (*silently and in slow motion*) become so angry that you _____. (*Let students choose how they want this pantomime to culminate: e.g., blow up in a puff of smoke, stamp through the floor, or split in two.*)

Narrative Pantomime

- You are the miller's daughter, seated in a room full of straw and ordered to spin it into gold. There isn't much you can do but try. But you can't get the straw to spin into gold. It's so hopeless, you begin to weep. Suddenly you hear a noise that startles you. You look up and see a strange little man. Dry your tears.

- You are the queen's messenger sent to find unusual names in the kingdom. You ride your horse through the woods and come upon a high hill. In the distance you see a little house with a fire in front of it and a little man dancing around on one foot chanting a verse. Rein in your horse and dismount. Go as close as you can without being seen or heard and listen. How will you react?

Solo Verbal Activities
Verbal Solo

- You're the miller's daughter who has been commanded to spin the straw into gold. You know straw can't be spun into gold, don't you? Why did you let your father talk you into this?

- You are the miller's daughter who is now a queen. How could you marry such a terrible man as the king seems to be? Didn't he really marry you for all the gold you produced for him? Didn't he also threaten to kill you if you didn't spin the straw into gold? How can you be happy with such a man?

- Rumpelstiltskin, why do you want the queen's baby? She offered you riches; why wouldn't you take that instead? Surely you are an honorable man and would not do the child any harm—but why does having this child means so much to you? Can you explain yourself?

- You are the queen's messenger, sent out to find names. Tell about the strange sight you saw in the woods. Don't leave out any details.

- You are the miller. That was quite a story you told about your daughter. What else can this unusual daughter of yours do?

Paired and Group Pantomime Activities
Mechanical Movement

- (*Do in groups of four.*) Become a spinning wheel that spins the straw into gold. As the music plays (*"Spinning Song"*), demonstrate how you work.

Count/Freeze Pantomime

- There are a lot of things to do in caring for babies. Pantomime one for us to guess.

- Rumpelstiltskin gave the queen three days to guess his name. What do you suppose he did while he was waiting for the three days to be up? Act out your idea for us to guess.

Pantomime Spelling

- Think of some other unusual names. Then spell them out, using a category (e.g., occupations or action words) your group agrees on.

(Vary the size of the groups so that the names won't all have the same number of letters in them.)

Build a Place

- Create Rumpelstiltskin's little hut. What sorts of things would he have in it? Do you think he has made provisions for the baby he thinks he is going to get? Is there anything magical in it?

Paired and Group Verbal Activities

Improvised Scene

- *(Do in pairs.)* Create the meeting between the miller and the king that led to the miller's claim that his daughter could spin straw into gold. Include in the scene the purpose of the miller's visit to the king in the first place.

- The miller has just told the king his daughter can spin straw into gold. Now he is afraid that he has bragged a little too much. How will he tell his daughter what he's done? How will she respond?

Leader in Role

- *(You play the queen.)* I desperately need some help in thinking of all the unusual names a person can have. It's the only way I can save my baby. Will you help me make a list of all the different names you can think of?

- *(You play a servant of Rumpelstiltskin's.)* Dear friends of Rumpelstiltskin, I know you share my master's happiness. I'm sure he will be getting the queen's baby any day now. I've invited you to this baby shower and we're now ready to see the special gifts you've brought for this very special baby. Please tell everyone who you are and what you have brought.

- *(You read a letter from Rumpelstiltskin.)* "Dear friends, I'm very sure that soon I shall have a baby to take care of. Would you make a list of things I will need to get for a baby? I would also like a list of all the things you think I should know about babies. Thank you. Very sincerely, A Friend. P.S. Leave your lists on the window sill." *(This activity might be done as two separate tasks. Or, half the class, in small groups, might be assigned to the first task; the other half to the second task.)*

Experts

- *(The experts know all about spinning straw into gold.)* Questions that might be asked: How do you spin the straw into gold? How did you learn to do it? What is the best kind of straw to use? Can the process be reversed?

Debate

- The queen tries to talk Rumpelstiltskin out of the awful bargain she made. How can she get him to change his mind? She tries other offers or deals, but Rumpelstiltskin seems firm. Will an offer be made that is too tempting for him to resist?

- The queen made a promise to Rumpelstiltskin and is trying to get out of honoring it. Rumpelstiltskin demands that she be held to the bargain. (*Double- or triple-cast volunteers in these two roles.*) The rest of you will be the people of the kingdom. You have been asked to solve the problem to the satisfaction of both sides. You are allowed to ask whatever questions you want of the queen and of Rumpelstiltskin. (*Afterward, divide the class into small groups to brainstorm solutions; keep queen and Rumpelstiltskin available for consultation. Have groups report their solutions. Check with both Rumpelstiltskin and the queen to see whether they can live with the decisions.*)

Related Activities

- You are newspaper columnists who have been asked to predict the future for a very greedy king married to a common miller's daughter. Write out your prediction and read it aloud.

- Research names and their meanings. Do you find any contradictions? What does your name mean? How do you feel about the meaning of your name? If you created a different or an unusual name for yourself, what might it be? What might be the meaning behind the name Rumpelstiltskin?

- Help Rumpelstiltskin write invitations to the baby shower and thank-you notes for the gifts received.

The Frog Prince

Jakob & Wilhelm Grimm

Summary: *A spoiled princess makes a bargain with a frog: If he finds her golden ball at the bottom of the well, she will let him be her companion, eat off her golden plate, and drink from her golden cup. Unknown to the princess, the frog is in reality a prince under a witch's spell. The kindness of the princess is needed to break the spell. However, as soon as the princess has her ball, she runs off to the palace. When the frog appears at the palace to remind the princess of her bargain, the king orders her to keep her promise. She does so reluctantly. The spell is finally broken (in a variety of ways, depending on the version), and the frog turns back into a prince who takes her to his kingdom to be his bride.*

Selected Picture Books

The Frog Prince. Translated by Naomi Lewis and illustrated by Binette Schroeder. North-South, 1989. A luminous quality surrounds the illustrations in this oversize edition.

The Frog Prince. Retold by Jan Ormerod and David Lloyd and illustrated by Jan Ormerod. Lothrop, Lee and Shepard 1990. Lavish illustrations incorporating medieval costumes and intriguing borders characterize this version.

The Frog Prince. Retold by Edith H. Tarcov and illustrated by James Marshall. Scholastic, 1987. The story is told with good-natured humor.

The Princess and the Frog. Written and illustrated by Rachel Isadora. Greenwillow, 1989. Watercolor illustrations with an intriguing use of shadows and light lend an immediacy to the tale.

Related Sources

The Frog Prince, Continued. Written by Jon Scieszka and illustrated by Steve Johnson. Viking, 1991. Forget "and they lived happily ever after." The Princess nags at the prince, who cannot give up old habits—like visiting the pond and eating flies. He searches for a witch to turn him back into a frog, but learns a lesson in love.

A Frog Prince. Written and illustrated by Alix Berenzy. Henry Holt, 1989. In this version the frog leaves the ungrateful princess and finds a lovely frog princess for his mate.

The Frog Princess. Retold by Elizabeth Isele and illustrated by Michael Hague. Crowell, 1984. In Russia, a czar orders each of his sons to shoot an arrow into the sky; they are then each to marry whoever finds his arrow. Ivan gets a frog, but underneath is a beautiful princess.

"The Marriage." Written by Sara Henderson Hay. From *Story Hour.* Doubleday, 1963. The queen says the groom isn't really a prince; her daughter is just a romantic.

Solo Pantomime Activities

Narrative Pantomime

- You are the princess, playing with your favorite toy, a golden ball. You throw it up in the air and catch it again and again. Whoops, you dropped it! Try to grab for it! Missed! There it goes, into the well. You try to see it in the deep water, but it's gone for good. Too bad. Not only was it beautiful, it was very valuable. You sit at the edge of the well. Show how you feel. As I count slowly to three, show what you might do next.

- You are the frog who has made the long journey by yourself to the palace to find the princess and make her keep her bargain with you. It has taken you an entire day and you are exhausted. Now you have reached a marble staircase, which you must climb. Show how you manage to do this. (*You might have them begin on the floor and when they reach the top step, they can sit at their desks. After they are all seated, say the final line.*) Don't forget that you have to knock at the door now that you've reached the top.

- You are the princess. Your father has ordered you to keep your promise to the frog, who has just asked to accompany you to your room. You pick him up with two fingers and carry him to your room. Show by your facial expression and the way you hold him how much you detest him. When you get to your room, put him in a corner so you won't have to look at him. What else can you do to hide him from view? (*Comment on what you see the students pantomiming, or discuss their ideas afterward.*)

Transformation and Slow-Motion Pantomime

• You are the frog. The princess has just thrown you against the wall and you change into a prince. Do this in slow motion to the count of ten.

Solo Verbal Activities

Verbal Solo

• You are the frog and have just retrieved the princess's golden ball. She has run off to the palace without taking you with her. Call to her in your croaky voice. One by one, let's hear what you would say.

Interview

• You're the king. Tell us, the night the frog appeared at the palace door, did you really think your daughter should have kept her promise? Were you embarrassed? Or, did you feel the need to show your power in front of the courtiers? Tell us your real feelings about this.

• You're the witch who turned the prince into a frog. Why would you do such a thing? What did he ever do to you?

• You're a courtier who was present at dinner when the frog came to the palace. From your point of view, did the king make too big an issue of his daughter's becoming friends with a frog? Explain your answer.

• You're the princess who married the frog prince. We hear he has found it difficult to adjust to human life again and feels the need to return to some of his old ways. Exactly what does he do that makes life so difficult for you?

• You're the prince who used to be a frog. We understand you're not happy with your life as it is at present. What is the worst problem you have being human again?

Storytelling

• You are the frog. You say a wicked witch turned you into your present state and you really are a prince. That seems a little hard for us to believe. Can you explain, in detail, how it happened and why?

Paired and Group Pantomime Activities

Improvised Scene

• The frog and the princess eat dinner off the same golden plate. The frog enjoys his meal immensely, but the princess is having problems carrying out her end of the bargain. Let's see some of this scene, which ends when the frog has had his fill.

Build a Place

• Suppose the frog spends several weeks in the palace before he changes into a prince. During that time, he expects to have certain adjustments made for him concerning living arrangements. Create a room for him, equipping it with things he would find necessary and desirable.

Count/Freeze Pantomime

• (Do this exercise in pairs.) The frog wants to play games with the princess. Besides throwing and catching a ball, pantomime some other games they could play. Remember their size difference and make any needed adjustments. (Example: They could play see-saw, but the frog would have to have extra weight on his end. What would he use?)

Paired and Group Verbal Activities

Improvised Scene

• The king questions the princess about her distress after answering the door and shutting it again. He wants to know who is at the door. She tries not to tell the story about the frog, but must give her father some answer that will satisfy him. What will she say? Will he believe her?

• The frog wishes to go sightseeing in the palace and asks the princess to guide him. She obliges only because the frog threatens to tell her father if she doesn't. Let's see a little of this scene, with the princess trying to cut the tour short and the frog wanting to see every nook and cranny. He also asks a lot of questions.

Debate

• The king and queen are having an argument about their youngest daughter and the difficulty she has keeping her promises. The king feels that as a princess she should exhibit model behavior, but the queen feels she is still too young to have such unreasonable demands made of her.

Experts

- The frog is very happy at the palace but wants to appear more human. He thinks clothes are the answer. A panel of clothing designers have been summoned to the palace to explain their ideas for dressing a frog. The king's advisers are questioning them. There's also the matter of cost.

- The king and queen are concerned that the princess could get warts from the frog. They have called in some specialists who can speak to the topic and perhaps offer suggestions for any possible cures—just in case. The king and queen will ask the questions.

Related Activities

- The frog is living happily at the palace when a letter arrives. It is from his friends back at the well, who wish to live at the palace, too. What does the letter say?

- The frog answers the letter from his friends. Will he encourage them to join him, or will he tell them stories that will discourage them? Write the letter for him.

- Design and sketch some of the frog clothing suggested in the experts game. Create a catalogue of clothing, complete with descriptions and prices.

- What other stories are there that have frogs or toads in them? Make two separate lists, distinguishing between the animals that talk and those that do not.

- In the original story, the princess simply threw the frog against the wall and he changed into a prince. In other versions, he changes only after she agrees to marry him; or she has to kiss him to break the spell; or he sleeps on her pillow for three nights. Rewrite the ending of the story and include a different way to break the spell.

- The princess is rude to the helpful frog. Apparently she needs some help behaving properly. Create a book of manners for the princess to follow.

- Write a newspaper society-column account of the wedding of the princess to the prince who used to be a frog. What might be said about his side of the family?

King Midas and
The Golden Touch

A Greek Myth

Summary: *King Midas, who loves gold more than anything else in the world, is granted his wish: the golden touch. The king is deliriously happy until he discovers that food and even his own beloved daughter also turn to gold at his touch.*

Selected Picture Books

The Golden Touch. Written by Nathaniel Hawthorne and illustrated by Paul Galdone. McGraw-Hill, 1959. The black-and-white drawings are enhanced with the colors orange and metallic gold.

King Midas and the Golden Touch. Retold and illustrated by Kathryn Hewitt. Harcourt, Brace, Jovanovich 1987.

King Midas and the Golden Touch. Retold by Freya Littledale and illustrated by Daniel Horne. Scholastic, 1989. Some modernization is apparent in this edition.

Related Sources

The Chocolate Touch. Patrick Skene Catling. Morrow, 1979. In this novel-length story, a young boy named John Midas is given the "chocolate touch." When his mother turns to chocolate mousse, he has second thoughts.

Favorite Greek Myths. Retold by Mary Pope Osborne and illustrated by Troy Howell. Scholastic, 1989. In this anthology's version of the story, it is Bacchus, god of the vine, who gives Midas his wish.

Solo Pantomime Activities

Narrative Pantomime

- King Midas loves to pass the time in a dungeonlike treasure room in the basement of his palace. Be King Midas, walking (*in place*) down the long, dark, winding stairway to the dungeon. You arrive at the door, carefully unlock it with a big key, enter, and carefully lock it again. Pick up a bag of gold coins and take it over to the one bright and narrow sunbeam that falls from a small window. Examine the coins, one by one, and whisper to yourself about how happy you are with your wealth.

- You are King Midas waking up, eager to test your golden touch to see if it is true. With joyful frenzy, you touch everything around you and watch as it changes to gold. Now touch the bedpost; a book (*the print becomes illegible*); put on clothes (*the weight is heavy*); Marygold's handkerchief (*you wish it hadn't changed*); spectacles (*you cannot see out of them*)—but in spite of all this, you still enjoy having the golden touch.

- Now you are King Midas trying to eat your breakfast. First you are surprised to discover that as soon as you touch your spoonful of coffee to your lips it turns to gold. Well, no matter, you will try one of the nice little trout on your plate—but it turns to a little golden fish. The same happens to one of the hot cakes you try to eat. You still can't believe what is happening, and you are now more concerned about getting something to eat than in having the golden touch. You reach for a boiled egg, which also turns to gold. With envy, you watch Marygold eating her breakfast. You try to cram a hot potato into your mouth quickly before it can turn to gold, but the solid hot metal burns your mouth terribly. You jump up and stamp about with pain and finally fall exhausted into your golden chair.

- Be Marygold, turned into a statue, your face bearing a questioning look of love, grief, and pity for your father. Now feel the handfuls of water King Midas is sprinkling over you. You come back to life again. Let us see the first thing you do.

- Be Midas jumping into the water, clothes and all, to rid yourself of the golden touch. You notice your clothes and the pitcher have changed from gold back to normal. Dip the pitcher in the water and hurry back to the palace. Pour it first over Marygold, then the roses, then everything else you turned into gold earlier. Even your heart now seems lighter.

• You are Marygold, trying to pick a bouquet of heavy golden flowers from your father's rose garden. You discover they have no fragrance and the hard petals prick your nose. Toss them aside in disgust.

Solo Verbal Activities

Verbal Solo

• You are one of King Midas's parents. What was he like as a child? Can you tell us when you first noticed his obsession with gold? Why gold rather than silver, jewels, or other valuable materials?

• You are King Midas. I have the power to grant your wish, but first you must convince me that giving you the golden touch will make you happy. (*You can respond as the stranger.*)

• Now, King Midas, the golden touch has been removed, as you requested. What advice would you give to someone who craves gold as much as you once did?

• Marygold, what differences do you notice in your father's behavior now that the golden touch has been removed? What does he do now that he didn't do before? What did he do before that he doesn't do now?

Paired and Group Pantomime Activities

Intragroup Pantomime

• Pantomime as many things as you can think of that are made of gold.

Statue

• Be people in the castle who were turned to gold when they accidentally came into contact with King Midas. The audience will try to guess what you were doing at the moment you were turned to gold.

Transformation and Slow-Motion Pantomime

• In pairs, one of you is a statue of gold, the other has a pitcher of water to restore the statue to his or her original state. As I count to ten, do this action in slow motion.

Build a Place

- Create the king's treasure room in the basement of the castle. What things might be stored there? What sorts of gold items might it have in it?

Paired and Group Verbal Activities

Debate

- King Midas's advisers debate whether or not he should keep his golden touch. One side argues that the kingdom could really use the money, while the other side is more concerned about the king's physical and emotional condition. What is the final decision?

Interview

- (*Have several children each play the young stranger, answering questions from the class.*) Who are you? Where did you come from? How did you know King Midas wanted the golden touch? Why did you give the golden touch to him? What if he decided to have it again, would you give it to him? Have you ever given the golden touch to other people? What did you expect King Midas to learn from having the golden touch? What other wishes can you grant?

- King Midas, his daughter, and three servants hold a press conference with reporters who are asking for details on the golden touch incident. Reporters, be diplomatic, please. The King is feeling embarrassed about the recent happenings and would like to forget the whole matter as soon as possible.

- It is now many years later, and King Midas's grandchildren sing an old song that tells the story of the golden touch. Create the song in groups of three and sing it for us. (*Use a simple tune such as "Twinkle, Twinkle Little Star."*)

Improvised Scene

- Suppose someone comes to visit King Midas while he has the golden touch. Midas has just realized his situation is more embarrassing than wonderful. How does he explain the presence of all the gold to his curious guest? And how will King Midas be hospitable while trying to avoid touching anything—including his guest?

Storytelling

- *(Do in groups of five.)* Create a brief story of what might happen in a modern setting if someone desired a wish like a chocolate touch, for example. *(Use this as an introduction to Patrick Skene Catling's* The Chocolate Touch.)

Related Activities

- Write an entry in Marygold's diary, detailing the events of the day when her father received and lost the golden touch.

- Find other stories that have wishes in them. Make a list of wishes that are granted in stories and wishes that are not. What is the success rate on wishes granted? How do the wish makers feel when their wishes are granted?

- The King wants to be sure he has changed everything back to its original state. Help the servants by making an inventory of all the things King Midas turned into gold.

- Research the subject of alchemy.

- King Midas has just discovered that the objects he turned into gold are plated, not solid. He wants to notify the public to be wary of a con artist claiming to be able to turn items into gold. Write a newspaper article, detailing the story and including the caution.

Snow White

JAKOB & WILHELM GRIMM

Summary: *A young princess is forced into hiding when her stepmother, the queen, becomes so jealous of the princess's beauty that the stepmother is determined to kill the princess. Snow White, as the princess is called, finds a home with seven dwarfs who mine gold for a living. The queen, through the aid of a magic mirror, finds where Snow White is hiding. Disguising herself as an old peddler woman, the queen eventually succeeds in poisoning Snow White with an apple. The dwarfs, who cannot bear to put her in the ground, place her in a glass coffin. A prince discovers her and begs the dwarfs to let him take her to his castle. As his servants carry the coffin away, the apple is dislodged from her throat and Snow White is returned to life. She marries the prince, and the wicked queen is forced to dance in red-hot iron shoes until she dies.*

Selected Picture Books

Snow White and the Seven Dwarfs. Translated and illustrated by Wanda Gag. Coward-McCann, 1938, 1965. Black-and-white lithographs with minute detail capture the folk quality of the tale.

Snow-White and the Seven Dwarfs. Translated by Randall Jarrell and illustrated by Nancy Ekholm Burkert. Farrar, Straus and Giroux, 1972. The hauntingly beautiful and lavishly detailed illustrations received the Caldecott Medal.

Snow White and the Seven Dwarfs. Retold by Freya Littledale and illustrated by Susan Jeffers. Scholastic, 1989. This is an easy-reader edition of the story.

Snow White. Translated by Paul Heins and illustrated by Trina Schart Hyman. Little, Brown, 1974. The translation is freely done, and the illustrations lend a somewhat gloomy tone to the story.

Related Sources

"One of the Seven Has Somewhat to Say." Written by Sara Henderson
    Hay. From *Story Hour*. Doubleday, 1963. One of the dwarfs longs
    for the days when they lived in comfortable clutter; "she" is just too
    precise and meticulous.

"Snow White and the Seven Dwarfs." Written by Roald Dahl. From *Roald
    Dahl's Revolting Rhymes*. Knopf, 1983. The seven dwarfs are ex-
    jockeys who love to bet on horses. Snow White steals the magic
    mirror to get racing tips, and they all wind up millionaires.

Snow White in New York. Written by Fiona French. Oxford University
    Press, 1986. This version is set in the 1920s, complete with seven
    jazzmen. The magic mirror is replaced by the *New York Mirror*.

Solo Pantomime Activities

Pantomime Solo

• Be one of the snowflakes, falling like a feather, that Snow White's
    mother saw as she gazed out the window. (*This also works well as a
    quieting activity.*)

• Snow White enters the dwarfs' house to rest. But each of the beds she
    tries out has a problem with it—one is too hard, another too short,
    and so on. Not until she reaches the seventh bed does she find one
    suitable. What is wrong with each of the other beds? As I count to
    seven, you be Snow White trying out six beds, each with something
    wrong, until you find the one that suits you. There you will lie down
    and fall fast asleep.

• When the dwarfs discover Snow White sleeping, they don't want to
    wake her. So the seventh dwarf has to sleep one hour with each of his
    comrades through the night. You're that seventh dwarf. I'll count to
    seven as you show the difficulty you had getting rest that first night.
    Try to show a different problem each time you get into another bed.

• Snow White is making a new suit of clothes for one of the dwarfs. Let
    us see what part of the outfit you are making by the way you hold and
    work with it.

• The huntsman has delivered a wild boar's heart in place of Snow
    White's to the queen. It has been salted and cooked for her. You are
    the queen, eating it smugly, thinking how clever you are to have rid
    yourself of your rival. Now laugh a silent, evil laugh.

• On the count of ten, you will be the queen going through all the steps she takes to disguise herself as an old peddler woman. We know she painted her face and dressed in old woman's clothes. What else does she do?

• When the queen hears for the last time that she is not the fairest of all, she is beside herself with envy and anger. You are the queen, experiencing this intense rage—but silently and in slow motion. As I count to ten you will hear the mirror's words, be overcome with anger by degrees, and finally sink in exhaustion to the floor.

• You are the queen, forced to dance in red-hot iron shoes at the wedding. As the music plays, you will begin to dance reluctantly, but soon the shoes take over and carry you along in a frenzy. When the music stops, you will collapse in slow motion to your death on the floor as I count to three. (*Use Khachaturian's "Sabre Dance," a tarantella, or other intense music.*)

Transformation

• You are the beautiful, proud queen. Slowly, as I count to ten, show us your evil side by becoming wicked and witchlike.

Solo Verbal Activities

Verbal Solo

• You are the queen's magic mirror. Tell us, how do you know who is the fairest one in the kingdom? What other things do you know? What do you really think about the queen? What would you like to say to her if you could?

• You are Snow White's father. What are your reasons for marrying the new queen? She doesn't seem at all like the former queen, does she? How do you feel about that?

Paired and Group Pantomime Activities

Improvised Scene

• (*Do in groups of eight.*) After the huntsman leaves Snow White, she walks through the woods trying to find her way. The trees almost seem to be alive, reaching out to her and trying to scare her. One of you is Snow White and the other seven are trees. As I play the music, let's see this scene. The trees must not actually touch Snow White. (*Suggested music: "Night on Bald Mountain" by Mussorgsky.*)

Count/Freeze Pantomime

- Snow White agrees to do all the housekeeping for the little men. Think of a chore she might do that we can guess. Remember that everything in the house is small.

Build a Place

- Create the little men's cottage. Remember that they are gold miners and all the items in the house are small. Be careful you don't hit your head on the low doorway as you go in and out.

Improvised Scene

- The little men arrive home and find Snow White asleep in bed. They decide to let her sleep while they quietly wash up and fix supper for themselves. But with seven, this could be difficult. Show how this scene might look. (*Do this in groups of seven. You might delineate a confined space and hand out cards with specific tasks written on them: chop wood, arrange tablecloth and napkins, place plates and cups, place silver, make tea, bake bread, cook porridge.*)

- (*Do this in groups of four.*) Be the prince's servants carrying Snow White's coffin down from the mountain. Lift it carefully, begin your journey, travel over rough stones, move through a wooded area, cross a stream with stepping stones, and finally reach the bottom, then set it down reverently. Go slowly and be sure to maintain the illusion of the coffin by remaining the same distance from each other as you move about. (*Pastoral music would help the mood.*)

- The dwarfs set Snow White's glass coffin on a mountain and watched over it. (*Place two chairs to represent the coffin.*) Birds came to mourn. Perhaps others did, too. One by one, you may come to pay your respects. As you come forward, you will also leave some token of remembrance. (*Soft music will help sustain the mood. Suggestion: Debussy's "La Mer," "Clouds," or "Claire de Lune."*)

Paired and Group Verbal Activities

Leader in Role

- (*You play the stepmother in disguise. Tell the children to pretend they are at home alone in the dwarfs' cottage.*) Hello, is anyone home? I have some lovely wares to sell. Come to the door so I can show you. (*Continue to entice the children to let you in. You will need to make excuses why you cannot show your wares through the window. Nor can you slip something under the door or leave samples. Be sure to keep the illusion of a door separating you from them; avoid making eye contact. Don't playact being scary; children will know who you are pretending to be. Though some individual children may entertain the notion of letting you in, the group probably will not allow it. Eventually you will need to give up, saying something like "Drat, foiled again," so they will know they have won. Return to the group as yourself and debrief them on their feelings.)*

- (*You pretend to be one of the little men.*) My brothers have asked me to come to you for help. We are concerned because Snow White isn't cautious enough and keeps letting strangers in the house. We've warned her about the wicked queen, but she is so trusting. What can we do? Can you list some ideas for us or help us with some plan? (*Let the children ask questions if they need to, or divide them into groups to brainstorm ideas.*)

- (*You are Snow White.*) I have a problem I don't know how to solve. As you know, some very nice gentlemen are letting me live in their home. In exchange for their generosity, I keep house for them. But seven people are a lot to cook and clean for, even if they are little. I think I'm being overworked, but I'm afraid to say anything. I don't want to hurt their feelings. What can I do?

Conversation

- Two castle servants are doing their work and talking about the king's new wife, comparing her with the late queen. They have noticed things about her that are strange and frightening. As we listen in on their conversation, what are they saying?

- The dwarfs are trying to decide on a wedding present for Snow White. What would be the most appropriate gift for them to give? Make a list of possibilities and see if you can agree on one. (*Use groups of seven.*)

Improvised Scene

- The king wonders where Snow White is; the queen fabricates a story about what happened in the woods. He probes for details, finding her story difficult to believe. Let's hear some of that conversation, which ends when the king seems satisfied with the information.

- The queen questions the mirror about who is the fairest in the land. The mirror is afraid to tell the truth and tries to change the subject. What happens next?

Interview

- You are some of the queen's servants who are willing to talk for a price. Questions that might be asked: What are some of the magic spells and tricks the queen uses? How does one get to the "secret lonely chamber" where she made the poisoned apple? Where did the magic mirror come from? Why is it so important to the queen to be the fairest in the land?

- After the wicked queen's death, several members of her family ask for an audience with the people of the kingdom in order to explain that she really liked Snow White and meant her no harm. What questions will the people ask? What will the queen's relatives answer in order to salvage her reputation?

Debate

- After the wedding, Snow White wants to invite the dwarfs to come and live in the palace. The prince doesn't think the idea is a good one. What will your final decision be?

Who Am I?

- Many children are so familiar with the Walt Disney version of the story, they assume his naming of the dwarfs is in the original version of the story. If they insist on including these identities in the playing, this game can be useful. By the way they answer questions, the audience must figure out who of the panel members is Grumpy, Dopey, Sneezy, Sleepy, Bashful, Doc, and Happy.

Related Activities

- Suppose the little men become so accustomed to having someone cook and clean for them that they decide to get a housekeeper. Write a newspaper advertisement for them, detailing their needs.

- Snow White writes a letter to the little men, inviting them to the palace for a visit. What interesting activities does she have planned for them?

- Prepare the wicked queen's book of magic spells.

- The dwarfs have a very orderly plan for keeping house before Snow White comes to live with them. Make out their "duty roster," indicating all the chores to be done for one week and who will do which ones.

- The dwarfs are so concerned about Snow White's encounters with the queen's poisonous spells they decide to write out a list of first-aid safety tips for her. Help them in this task.

The Sleeping Beauty

Charles Perrault

Summary: *A king and queen invite fairies to their baby daughter's christening. However, one important fairy is overlooked, and she revengefully announces that the princess will one day prick her finger on the spindle of a spinning wheel and die. Although the curse cannot be overturned, a kind fairy changes it to a hundred-year sleeping spell. Furthermore, the princess is to be rescued by a prince who awakens her with a kiss. All comes true as predicted. When the princess is sixteen, she has her accident with a spinning wheel. The good fairy is informed and returns to cast the hundred-year sleeping spell over all the inhabitants of the palace so that the princess would not be alone upon awakening. After a hundred years, a prince braves the dense brambles that no man or beast has been able to penetrate and rescues the princess. The second episode of the French tale, which includes an ogress (Night) who eats Beauty's children (Dawn and Day) and threatens Beauty (Sun), is generally omitted. The princess in the Grimm Brothers' version of this story is called Briar Rose. In Perrault's version of the story there are eight fairies, while the Grimm version has thirteen.*

Selected Picture Books

The Sleeping Beauty. Illustrated by Mercer Mayer. Macmillan, 1984. Rich colors and detail, with softening touches, characterize this beautifully executed work.

The Sleeping Beauty. Adapted by Jakob and Wilhelm Grimm and illustrated by Warwick Hutton. McElderry, 1979. Watercolor illustrations promote a tranquil mood.

The Sleeping Beauty. Retold and illustrated by Trina Schart Hyman. Little, Brown, 1983. In this retelling of the Grimm version, dark colors lend a somber mood.

The Sleeping Beauty. Translated and illustrated by David Walker. Crowell, 1976. Romantic watercolors in gold and bronze tones give a dream-like quality.

Related Sources

About the Sleeping Beauty. Written by P. L. Travers and illustrated by Charles Keeping. McGraw-Hill, 1975. Six versions of the tale are presented (including the author's own), along with an essay on the meaning in tales.

"The Sleeper." Written by Sara Henderson Hay. From *Story Hour*. Double-day, 1963. This poem, written in two parts, lets us hear the inner thoughts of Sleeping Beauty and the prince. She misses the privacy she had; he finds her to be stubbornly selfish.

Sleeping Beauty. Retold by C.S. Evans and illustrated by Arthur Rackham. Viking, republished 1972. This extended telling of the Grimm version takes eleven chapters and is illustrated in black-and-white silhouettes.

Sleeping Ugly. Written by Jane Yolen and illustrated by Diane Stanley. Coward-McCann, 1981. A beautiful but haughty princess, a plain girl, and a fairy fall into a hundred-year sleep. A poor prince awakens the girl and the fairy with a kiss and the sleeping princess sleeps on.

Solo Pantomime Activities

Slow-Motion Pantomime

- You are the young princess who pricks her finger on the spinning wheel's spindle and falls into a deep sleep. Do this in slow motion to the count of ten. (*Sidecoach: You are becoming sleepy, your eyelids are drooping, you're yawning, you can't hold your head up, etc.*)

- You are the dwarf messenger who informs the good fairy when the princess's deep sleep occurs. Put on your seven-league boots and run (*in place and in slow motion*) the twelve thousand leagues to find her. Remember, you can go seven leagues in one step.

Noiseless Sound

- Suppose someone is in the middle of a sneeze when the sleeping spell is cast. Let's try this in slow motion, with no sound, as I count to five. Then you will be frozen in time, in the middle of a sneeze. (*While they are frozen, tell them the spell will be broken when they hear the sound of a kiss. On that cue, they will wake up suddenly and complete the sneeze. Kiss the back of your hand loudly to cue.*)

Quieting Activity

• The entire castle is asleep, people and animals, everyone. Each one would look and sound a little different from everyone else. Decide on some person or animal you wish to be and take your sleeping position. The sleep will be so deep there will be no snoring or other sounds. As I play the music, let's see this enchanted sleep. (*Suggested music: "Sleeping Beauty Ballet" by Tchaikovsky.*)

Solo Verbal Activities

Verbal Solo

• The uninvited fairy grumbled about being slighted and even muttered some threats under her breath. What might this have sounded like?

• We know what Sleeping Beauty's first recorded words were upon awakening after her hundred years' sleep. Is it possible she might have said something else that didn't get recorded? What might those words have been?

• You're the person to whom the king assigned the task of destroying all the spindles in the kingdom. The king now wants to know how you missed the spindle that was in the castle's tower. What is your explanation?

Storytelling

• Over the years, many stories have been told about the far-off castle surrounded by thick woods that no one can penetrate. You live within sight of the castle. What stories have you heard?

Paired and Group Pantomime Activities

Improvised Scene

• (*Do this in pairs.*) The old woman spins fast. She's done it for years and for her it's very easy. She tries to teach Sleeping Beauty, but the princess has never even seen a spindle before. What would this scene look like in pantomime? It ends when Sleeping Beauty pricks her finger and falls slowly into her deep sleep.

- As I play music, slowly become the brambles that grow up and surround the castle. Be prickly and twisty, intertwining with one another, so that neither man nor beast can pass through you. (*Try this with everyone in a large circle.*)

Frozen Picture

- (*Divide the class into groups of eight.*) Let's see a christening photo of the eight fairies. Be sure we can tell who the uninvited fairy is.

- (*Divide the class into groups of three.*) In your group, create a frozen picture of different events that were taking place at the moment the spell was cast over you. (*Take time to note or guess what the events and characters are: e.g., grooms taking care of horses, cooks turning a spit, knights polishing armor, and so on.*) Now, let's enact the moment the spell is broken. As I count backwards from ten, you will slowly—remember you have been in the same position for a hundred years—return to pantomiming what you were doing before the spell was cast.

Count/Freeze Pantomime

- The palace has been standing a hundred years—with no cleaning or caretaking being done. Now a big cleanup begins. Think of someone you might be and what kind of task will you tackle after one hundred years of dirt has accumulated. We'll try to guess who you are and what your task is.

Mechanical Movement

- (*Divide the class into groups of five.*) Create a spinning wheel and demonstrate how it works.

Paired and Group Verbal Activities

Interview

- (*The interviewers may be reporters.*) You are the old woman in the tower who was spinning. Who are you? Why did you have a spinning wheel when the king had ordered them all destroyed? Did you also fall asleep during the spell?

- (*The interviewers may be reporters.*) We've heard that the princess dreamed of the prince while she was asleep. You are a person in the kingdom or a resident of the palace. Who are you and what dream did you have during the hundred years you slept?

Debate

- The king and queen disagree whether they should tell their daughter, who is now fifteen years old, of the spell cast upon her as a baby. The king thinks she should be informed; the queen wants to protect her from the news. Who will convince whom?

- (*Use groups of four.*) The two servants in charge of all the cleaning request an audience with the princess and her new husband. They complain of all the work that needs to be done after a hundred years of neglect, and ask for more assistance in the way of staff and supplies. The young couple are not sure this is necessary and feel that, in due time, all will be put right again. Besides, they will be moving to the prince's palace before long. What other reasons for frugality might be given and how will the servants respond?

Leader in Role

- (*You play a servant of the king and queen.*) The king and queen wish to have all the fairies in the kingdom be godmothers for the new princess. The trouble is finding them. What do you know about where fairies live or how we could get word to them? There's even one who hasn't been seen in fifty years. Do you have any ideas of her whereabouts?

- (*You play a servant of the prince.*) The prince is embarrassed to kiss Sleeping Beauty because he really doesn't know her at all. They haven't even been introduced. I think she's a bit too dusty for kissing anyway. You're wizards who know all sorts of spells. What else might he do to break this sleeping spell?

- (*You play a worried court official.*) The people in the court are all arguing about whether a wedding invitation should be sent to the fairy who cast the spell on Sleeping Beauty. Some say she doesn't deserve to be invited and others are afraid she might feel slighted and cast another spell. What do you think we should do?

- (*You play a worried court official.*) We've a bit of a problem and the king has asked for your help. You see, one of the persons in the castle didn't wake up when the spell was undone. What should we do about this person? (*The person may be some lesser, nonspecific official with no family that anyone knows about.*)

Conversation

- (*Use groups of five, six, or seven.*) The good fairies are disgruntled. All the attention is centered on the old fairy who cast the evil spell. Everyone seems to have forgotten their special gifts to the princess. What does their conversation sound like?

- (*Use groups of five.*) The people of the kingdom are complaining about having to do away with their spinning wheels and the great inconvenience this will create for them, especially those whose livelihood depends on spinning. Let's hear some of their conversation.

- (*Use pairs.*) The old man tells the prince of the story of the enchanted princess. The prince is determined to find her in spite of the old man's warnings of what had happened to other princes. How might this conversation sound?

- (*Use pairs.*) After the spell is broken, a kitchen servant continues his tasks of preparing food and cleaning in the kitchen, not realizing he was asleep for a hundred years. One of the prince's servants is trying to tell him what happened, but the servant is very puzzled and finds such a story hard to believe.

- (*Use pairs.*) The king tries to apologize to the old fairy for not inviting her, but she does not forgive easily. What excuses will he give and what will the fairy say in return?

- (*Use pairs.*) Sleeping Beauty is having her wedding dress designed, but her style is out of date. After all, even the prince noticed that her only dress looks like one his great grandmother would have worn. The bridal consultant tries diplomatically to interest her in the new styles. What will Sleeping Beauty's reaction be to the latest designs?

Interview Panel

- (*Panel members impersonate the wicked fairy.*) Some questions that might be asked: The king and queen couldn't find you, since nobody had seen you for fifty years; where have you been? Why did it bother you so much not having the same dinner service as the other fairies? Why would you cast such a horrible spell on a baby? What is your relationship to the other fairies?

Experts

- You are royal marriage counselors. Although the princess is the same age as the prince, there is a hundred years' difference in their backgrounds. What problems might this create and are they solvable? What predictions do you have for the success of this marriage?

Related Activities

- The king and queen have come to you for assistance in planning the big celebration for the christening. They've invited the fairies in the kingdom, but they have no idea what fairies eat. Plan a menu for the fairies that will please their delicate sensibilities.

• Prepare a program for the christening and/or the wedding. What events are listed? Who are the participants? How will the program be decorated?

• Create a book of magic spells related to sleep.

• Search for other stories with sleeping spells in them.

• Write a toast to be said at the wedding of Sleeping Beauty and the prince.

• Write a script for a modern television announcer, reporting the discovery of the legendary sleeping princess.

• Write the king's proclamation that no one is allowed to spin with a distaff and spindle, or even *have* a spindle.

• The princess wants to know what she has missed in the last hundred years during her sleep. Write a brief history (or create a timeline), indicating what you believe to be the most important events that have taken place in her country and in the world.

Beauty and the Beast

A FRENCH TALE

Summary: *A merchant loses his way on his journey home and stumbles upon a castle inhabited by a beast. The merchant takes a rose from the castle garden for his daughter Beauty. Although the beast demands the merchant's life for the theft, he allows him to live if one of his daughters will take his place. Beauty courageously agrees to the trade and lives in the palace. When the beast asks her to marry him, however, she cannot consent. Although her stay at the palace is pleasant enough, she becomes homesick and asks to return to her family for a visit. The beast agrees, but says she must return within two months or he will die. During her absence, the beast almost expires. At home, Beauty misses the beast and arrives in time to break his curse of ugliness; forgetting his looks and thinking of his kind nature, she agrees to marry him. At that moment he turns into the prince she has dreamed about and they are happily married. (There are different versions of this lengthy tale. The drama activities presented here are based on the Andrew Lang version in* The Blue Fairy Book *(Longmans, 1889). The picture books present condensed tellings from various sources.)*

Selected Picture Books

Beauty and the Beast. Retold and illustrated by Jan Brett. Houghton Mifflin/ Clarion, 1989. The story is told with simplicity. Tapestries show the beast's castle personnel as they were before the spell was cast.

Beauty and the Beast. Retold and illustrated by Mordicai Gerstein. Dutton, 1989. Line drawings against a background of strong color allows the imagination to fill in detail.

Beauty and the Beast. Translated by Richard Howard and illustrated by Hilary Knight. Simon & Schuster, 1990. Elongated drawings are colorful and flat, reminiscent of the best of animated film.

Beauty and the Beast. Retold by Philippa Pearce and illustrated by Alan
    Barrett. Crowell, 1972. Small figures in gouache paintings create a
    mysterious impression.

Beauty and the Beast. Retold by Marianna Mayer and illustrated by Mercer
    Mayer. Four Winds, 1978. Elaborate illustrations with rich color
    lend enchantment to the story.

Beauty and the Beast. Retold and illustrated by Warwick Hutton. Atheneum,
    1985. These illustrations are watercolor paintings in muted tones.

Related Sources

"Sequel." Written by Sara Henderson Hay. From *Story Hour*. Doubleday,
    1963. Beauty shares the royal life with her husband but nostalgically
    wishes for the quiet, tender moments they had together when he was
    the beast.

Solo Pantomime Activities

Transformation

- You are a rosebud in the beast's flower garden. As the music plays,
  you will slowly bloom into the most exquisite rose Beauty's father has
  ever seen.

- You are the prince sitting on your throne. Now the curse is put on
  you and you slowly transform into an ugly beast. Get up and walk
  around your throne, moving as a beast might. Now the curse is
  slowly breaking and you transform back into the prince again.
  Return to your throne.

Solo Verbal Activities

Verbal Solo

- You are Beauty. Tell us, we who are your family, about your life at
  the beast's palace. Tell one thing you like about it and one thing you
  don't like. Also, explain why.

- You are the beast. Do you remember what happened to you? Who
  cast the spell on you and why? What are your feelings about it?

- You are Beauty's father. Justify your reasons for leaving your daughter with the beast instead of staying to take your punishment.

• Beauty, you know the beast is going to ask you—again—to marry him. What reason will you give this time for saying no. Remember that you don't want to hurt his feelings.

• You are the beast. Suppose Beauty has not returned as promised. Let us hear one thought you might have.

• You are one of Beauty's father's former business partners. Explain why you divided up the merchant's goods among yourselves. What do you intend to do now that you know he is alive?

• You are all rich former friends of Beauty and her family. Now that they are poor, you don't want to do anything with them. You've heard they are hoping you'll invite them to come and live with you. As we go around the room, give a one-sentence excuse for not being able to take them in. Although you say the words politely, there is a tinge of superiority in your voice.

• You're one of Beauty's sisters. Let's hear your explanation of why you think you shouldn't be the one to go to the beast's palace instead of Beauty.

Sound Effects

• Beauty's father goes into the huge palace and finds only a deep silence. Suppose that he calls out, "Is no one here?" and an echo answers him. What would that sound like? I'll be Beauty's father calling out, and you will be the echo. (*Divide the class into five or six groups and have each group repeat the echo, becoming softer and softer until the final group speaks barely in a whisper.*)

Paired and Group Pantomime Activities

Count/Freeze Pantomime

• Beauty's brothers and sisters pantomime something special they want their father to bring back for them. The rest of us will guess what it is you want.

Mechanical Movement

• The clock in Beauty's room must be very special if it wakes her up by calling her name out loud. Create this clock. As I point to you, give your group's version of how Beauty's name was called three times. (*Do this in groups of five.*)

Build a Place

- Beauty's family was well off and then became poor. Create a room in their house, furnished with beautiful items. After the room is finished, creditors will come and remove everything. Then Beauty's family will have to replace each item with a cruder one or something entirely different.

- At the beast's request, Beauty packs four boxes with rare and precious things from the castle to take as gifts to her family. What are some of the things she would pack? (*Outline four rectangles to represent the boxes.*)

Statue

- The beast's castle is very elegant, and there are many statues inside and around the palace grounds. What sorts of statue groupings might there be? (*Divide the class into groups of varying sizes.*)

Frozen Picture

- Show Beauty's family welcoming her back home for the visit. What are the various emotions each family member is feeling?

- Show two frozen pictures. The first will be of Beauty and her family while they had great wealth; the second will be after they have fallen into the direst poverty.

Mirroring

- (*Do in groups of five.*) You are in the room lined with mirrors. Your reflection seems to be all around you. One of you will be the person looking into four mirrors, which face you in a semicircle. All four mirrors will do what you do. Try on the beautiful clothes and jewels the beast has given to you. (*Students may be Beauty or one of the family members.*)

Improvised Scene

- Beauty and her father eat dinner in the palace. The servants tend to all their needs but are invisible. Let's see this scene as the servants wait on them but Beauty and her father do not see them at all. The scene ends when dinner is over.

- The merchant lost all his ships at sea because of pirate attack, shipwreck, or fire. Show one of these disasters. (*Divide the class into groups of five. Do as a shadow mime, using a sheet backlit with a bright light.*)

- Beauty had several dreams while she was in the beast's palace. Show one of these dreams. (*May be done as a shadow mime. Play ethereal music under the scene.*)

- Act out an amusing pantomime that Beauty might have watched in the beast's palace. (*May be done as a shadow mime. Suggested music: "The Comedians" by Kabalevsky.*)

Paired and Group Verbal Activities

Improvised Scene

- Beauty's father describes to his family what happened to him at the beast's palace. Beauty's brothers want to search out the beast and kill him, while her sisters say the trouble they're in is Beauty's fault because she asked for the rose. The scene ends when it is agreed that Beauty will go to the palace. (*Use groups of six.*)

- Beauty's brothers are planning a rescue attempt to get her from the beast's palace. What will their plan be and what will be needed to pull it off? Subtle cleverness—not violence—is the key.

Conversation

- Beauty's sisters are talking together about her being home for a visit. They find they have become accustomed to her not being at home and now she seems to be a bit in the way. Let's hear a bit of their whispered conversation.

Experts

- A panel of experts will try to explain the "disease" of ugliness. (*Select panel members who will treat the topic seriously.*) The beast (*the audience members*) will probably want to know what kinds of cures they would suggest.

- In pairs, one of you will be a talking bird from the aviary; the other will be an aviary keeper, who will demonstrate what is distinctive and different about this special bird. All the birds will be different from each other, although they all talk.

Interview

- Reporters interview the sisters at the wedding. How do they feel about having a sister who is now royalty? What other questions are asked? (*Do this in pairs.*)

Related Activities

• Write a story explaining how a prince would be turned into a beast. Who cast the spell and why? How will the spell be removed?

• Beauty and the beast often have second thoughts about their new life. What might each write in their diaries when they long for the life that used to be?

• The beast in this story is portrayed in different ways in the various versions as well as in artists' illustrations. Compare the written descriptions and artistic renditions of what a "beast" is. Which do the students prefer and why? Have them draw their own version of the beast.

• What other stories are known or can be found that have the theme of ugliness redeemed through the power of love?

The Fool of the World and the Flying Ship

A RUSSIAN TALE

Summary: *The czar announces that he will give his daughter's hand in marriage to anyone who brings him a flying ship. The two older sons in a peasant's family set off to try their luck but are never heard from again. The youngest son, even though he is made fun of by them all, decides to take on the challenge. With the help of an ancient wise man and some friends he meets along the way, the fool accomplishes his goal.*

Picture Book

The Fool of the World and the Flying Ship. Retold by Arthur Ransome and illustrated by Uri Shulevitz. Farrar, Straus and Giroux, 1968. The only picture book of this tale, it is also a winner of the Caldecott Medal.

Other Sources

Favorite Tales Told in Russia. Retold by Virginia Haviland and illustrated by Herbert Danska. Little, Brown, 1961.

Tales from Central Russia. Retold by James Riordan and illustrated by Krystyna Turska. Kestrel, 1976.

Solo Pantomime Activities
Pantomime Solo

 • You're the fool sitting with the ancient old man. He asks you to open the sack your mother packed for you and share your food with him. You are reluctant to do this because you are embarrassed by the poor food you have to offer. This changes to astonishment when you discover the wonderful food that appears miraculously in the sack. Show these changes of emotion as I count slowly to five.

Transformation

• Be a stick of wood, slowly transforming into a tall, strong soldier as I count to ten.

Solo Verbal Activities

Verbal Solo

• You're the czar. Why do you want a flying ship so badly that you are willing to give your daughter's hand in marriage for one?

• You're the princess. What do you think of marrying a man who invents a flying ship? Is that your idea of a good husband?

• The fool watches his brothers go off and wishes to do the same, in spite of his mother's scoffing. Over and over he says, "I am going." You're the fool. Let's see how many different ways that sentence might be said. (*In addition to varying intonations, children may wish to emphasize their words with pantomime.*)

• You're the fool's mother. What was that more important business you had to tend to that kept you from seeing your youngest son off on his journey? How do you feel now that he's married to the czar's daughter?

• You are the ancient old man who gave the fool the valuable information. Why did you share this knowledge with him? Couldn't you have obtained the ship yourself and married the czar's daughter?

• You are the man with his ear to the ground, "listening to all that is being done in the world." Tell us about one thing you hear.

Storytelling

• We are told the two clever brothers went off on their adventure and were never heard from again. Are there any rumors or stories about what might have happened to them? Tell us who you are and what you've heard.

• When the fool and his passengers in the flying ship arrive at the czar's palace, they sit around telling jokes. You're one of the passengers. What joke would you tell? Riddles are also allowed.

Paired and Group Pantomime Activities

Build a Place

• Build a peasant's hut, similar to the one the fool and his family may have lived in. What kinds of furniture or other items would be in such a hut in Russia?

• The fool and his new wife want to go on an adventure in the flying ship. Let's pretend we're their servants, loading the ship with the things they want to take with them. This will probably include food and clothing as well as any luxuries they think they cannot be without on their trip.

Frozen Picture

• Create pictures from the fool's family photo album. Show the family in some family activity or event. Show how the fool is somehow always in the least-noticed position (*e.g., behind someone, loaded down with items, or peeking from behind a curtain*).

• (*Do in groups of ten.*) Arrange a wedding photo to include the fool and the czar's daughter as well as all the fool's friends (the ancient old man, Listener, Swift-goer, Far-shooter, Eater, Drinker, Strawman, and Woodman.) Be sure we know who's who.

• Create frozen pictures of some of your favorite scenes in the story.

Count/Freeze Pantomime

• Be one of the fool's friends doing something appropriate to his unique characteristic. We'll try to guess who you are.

Paired and Group Verbal Activities

Interview Panel

• (*Use groups of six.*) The panel consists of the passengers (Listener, Swift-goer, Far-shooter, Eater, Drinker, Strawman, and Woodman) the fool picked up in his flying ship. They all have interesting characteristics and skills the audience wishes to ask about. Some questions that might be asked: How did you get your skill? What other situations have you been in when you found your particular skills useful? Specific questions may also be addressed to each.

- (*Use groups of six.*) Each panel member is the ancient old man. Some questions that might be asked: Where were you going when you met the fool? Did you have anything to do with the fine food the fool found in his pack? How did you know the secret to making a flying ship? Where did you go after you helped the fool? Why did you tell him to pick up everyone he saw along the way?

Experts

- You are experts on building flying ships. The audience is a gathering of people interested in purchasing such a wonder. Some may even be interested in buying more than one.

Improvised Scene

- (*Use groups of three.*) Now that the fool has married the czar's daughter, his parents are anxious to see him again. They arrive at the palace and pretend to be the loving parents they never were before. The fool is too fine a fellow to be rude to them, but clearly enjoys talking to them and seeing their changed behavior as they try to ingratiate him. Let us listen in on some of this conversation.

Who Am I?

- Pretend to be the fool's friends, and we will guess who's who. (*Use a group of six—or seven, if you include the ancient old man. Let the panel members draw cards with their identity on it. For older students, you might let them ask questions of all the panel members, then stop to guess all the characters at once. The guessers may work in groups to solve the problem.*)

Leader in Role

- (*You play a messenger from the fool.*) My master has asked me for your advice in a problem he has. All his friends have stayed at the palace, but now they are presenting some problems. When they get bored, they like to show off their special skills. But the eater and drinker are using up the food supply; the far-shooter is taking pot shots at targets in the neighboring country; the swift-goer creates traffic problems; the strawman creates cold weather wherever he goes; and the wood-man's soldiers are all about the palace. The czar's patience is wearing thin. What can my master do without offending his friends? I'd like for you to talk this over and let me know your ideas. I have some urgent business to attend to, but I'll be back in a little while for your suggestions.

Related Activities

- Write a merry song for the fool to sing as he goes off on his adventure, enjoying the green trees and blue sky. As an alternative, write new lyrics to an old song. (*"The Happy Wanderer" is a possibility.*)
- Write a song for the fool and the ancient old man to sing in happiness over the food and drink they share together.

- Make a list of songs suitable for singing in a flying ship; or write a new one for the fool and his passengers.

- Create a model of the flying ship. Use balsa wood or cardboard cartons. Or make drawings of the flying ship, showing it from different angles and labeling all the necessary parts.

- The fool's parents write a letter of apology for the way they treated him and ask to come for a visit to his palace. How is the letter worded?

- The fool writes a letter back to his parents telling of his adventures. What else might he say?

- Write a story about how one (or more) of the fool's friends helped him out of trouble on another occasion after his marriage to the czar's daughter. (*Some of the students' stories might lend themselves to dramatization.*)

- Write a story about one of the fool's brothers' adventure. Will it be a successful story—as successful as the fool's—or will he have a difficult time making his way in the world? (*Again, some of these stories might lend themselves to dramatization.*)

- After the fool married the czar's daughter, he "became so clever that all the court repeated everything he said." Make a list of some of the clever things the fool has said that would be worth repeating.

The Jolly Tailor Who Became King

A POLISH TALE

Summary: *When a gypsy predicts that a very thin but jolly tailor will become king if he goes westward, he sets off on his journey. With the help of a scarecrow, he manages to frighten off dogs and devils until he reaches the rain-drenched city of Pacanow. He solves the problem by sewing up a hole in the sky and then marries the late king's daughter as his reward.*

Selected Sources

Favorite Fairy Tales Told in Poland. Retold by Virginia Haviland and illustrated by Felix Hoffman. Little, Brown, 1963.

The Jolly Tailor and Other Fairy Tales. Translated from the Polish by Lucia Merecka Borski and Kate B. Miller and illustrated by Kazimir Klepacki. Longmans, 1928, 1956.

Solo Pantomime Activities

Pantomime Solo

- You are Mr. Joseph Nitechka, the thinnest tailor of all. It is said you are so thin you can pass through the eye of your own needle. Would you show us how that is done, please?

- The tailor eats noodles, as they are the only food which can pass down his throat. You will probably need to eat them one at a time and they'll have to go down lengthwise. Let's see you doing that as I count to three, one count for each of three noodles.

- You are the nobleman the jolly tailor meets. You are warming yourself by your fireplace, eating a glowing coal from time to time. Show how you do this and how pleasurable it is, since you are in actuality a devil.

Narrative Pantomime

- You are the scarecrow. You walk with great dignity, but you are made of straw with sticks for hands and feet. Let's see how you look walking across the field. Now some dogs are coming at you, so you take off one of your feet and throw it at them to scare them away. You retrieve your foot and tie it back on and go on your way. Brave scarecrow!

- You are the tailor saving the town from the deluge. Carefully get your one hundred needles together, your thimbles, and your iron. Thread one needle from the huge spool of thread the scarecrow is holding. Go up the long ladder until you reach the sky. You sew for two days, wearing out one needle after another. Your fingers are stiff and you are very tired, but you do not stop. Finally the hole is sewn up and you press it carefully with the iron. Now you can climb down. You sit at the bottom of the ladder, extremely exhausted but well satisfied with your work.

Solo Verbal Activities

Verbal Solo

- You are the gypsy who cut her foot. Tell us how the accident happened and how you felt when Mr. Nitechka sewed your wound so carefully that no scar shows. Can you also tell us how you knew he would be king?

- You are the old man who tells the tailor that the west must be where the sun sets. Can you tell us how you know that is so? What other bits of wisdom have you learned in your lifetime of one hundred and six years that you could share with us?

- You are the daughter of the family that lives in the walking house. Let us hear her laughter that sounds like a horse neighing in the meadow. Does she also throw her head back like a horse would?

- You are the cook for the walking-house family. What problems do you encounter when gathering the ingredients and preparing the food? What other specialties do you make?

• When Mr. Nitechka suddenly figured out how the hole got in the sky he "gave a cry of joy like a goat's bleating." How would that sound?

• The tailor-king has made you, the scarecrow, the great warden of the kingdom. Your job is to keep sparrows away from the king's head. Tell us about your work. What is a typical day like?

Paired and Group Pantomime Activities

Improvised Scene

• When Mr. Nitechka greets someone, he bows and hops up and down three times, as he believes well-bred gentlemen should do. In pairs, be Mr. Nitechka greeting another well-bred person.

• The tailor mends the scarecrow's clothes so that he looks neat and handsome. Let's see that, remembering the skill the tailor has.

• The family in the walking house invite Count Scarecrow and Mr. Nitechka to join them for a meal of hot pitch, rats in black sauce, fried locust, lobster worms with Parmesan cheese like noodles, and old bad eggs. The family enjoys the meal immensely, but Count Scarecrow and Mr. Nitechka only pretend to eat while throwing the food under the table. Show this scene, including the strange-looking servant. Don't forget that the scarecrow and tailor become more and more frightened as the meal progresses. The scene will be over when the host announces that the king of Pacanow has died. (*Assign from five to eight students to each group. You might list the food courses on the chalkboard in the order they are served.*)

Mirror Game

• On holidays, the tailor braids his beard of one hundred and thirty-six hairs. Pretend it is a holiday and you are doing just that in front of a mirror. Be sure no hair gets left out.

Build a Place

• We know that the walking-house family was always cold. They had a blazing fire in summer, ate live coals, and sat on iron pots filled with glowing coals. Build a house for them, making sure everything in it will help them keep warm.

• (*Do in groups of six.*) Create your version of the house that could walk. Show how it dances in the forest. (*Play lively music by Shostakovitch.*)

- (*Do in groups of four.*) Be the townspeople who gather up all the ladders in the town. You tie them all together and lean the one huge ladder against the sky. (*Have the groups discuss their plan first, then execute it in pantomime.*)

Paired and Group Verbal Activities

Leader in Role

- (*You play the tailor.*) Greetings, my friends of the town of Pacanow. You've asked me to help you stop the rain, but I need to know how bad the problem is and what measures you've already taken to stop it. Who wishes to speak first? (*End by saying you need a few days to think of a plan of your own.*)

Debate

- The citizens of Pacanow notice that since the tailor sewed up the hole in the sky, their town is getting no rain at all. The flowers, trees, and gardens in their once lovely city have dried up. They take their complaints to the new king and his advisers, who think the town is doing just fine in the constant sunshine. What reasons will both sides give for their point of view?

Interview

- The jolly tailor is interviewed by a reporter who wants to know what qualifications he has for being a king. What will he be able to do for the people of Pacanow?

- Suppose that after the jolly tailor becomes king, he sends for the gypsy who predicted his fate. He asks her to predict his future again. What will she tell him this time, and how will he react to the news? (*Do this exercise in pairs.*)

Experts

- The town of Pacanow is famous for having smiths who shoe goats. Even the burghermaster rides on a shod goat. Let's have a panel of smiths who can tell us more about this profession.

Related Activities

- What other stories about tailors can be found?
- The tailor and the scarecrow became great friends. If they were to write about their friendship, what would they say?

• The scarecrow wanted to get married. Write a story about how he finds a suitable partner. Does his friend the tailor-king help him in any way?

• Now that the scarecrow has a responsible position in the government as great warden of the kingdom, he probably needs a nice uniform to go along with his job. Design and draw an appropriate uniform for him.

• Do research on the occupation of tailoring. How does the information help in understanding Mr. Nitechka's character?

The Nightingale

Hans Christian Andersen

Summary: *The emperor of China discovers that a little nightingale charms all who hear it sing, so much so that they are moved to tears. The emperor demands that it be brought to court, where it wins the hearts of all. But when a jeweled, mechanical bird is sent as a gift from the emperor of Japan, all attention turns to it and the little nightingale flies back to its home. In due time the mechanical bird wears out and, even though repaired, can only be played once a year. As time goes on, the emperor falls deathly ill. The nightingale returns to sing comforting songs to him, saves his life, and agrees to remain if he will be allowed to come and go as he wishes.*

Selected Picture Books

The Emperor and the Nightingale. Adapted by Joel Tuber and illustrated by Robert Van Nutt. Rabbit Ears, 1988. Handsome illustrations, colorful and detailed, capture the story's setting.

Hans Christian Andersen's The Nightingale. Translated by Eva Le Gallienne and illustrated by Nancy Ekholm Burkert. Harper, 1965. The setting is presented most handsomely, in exquisite detail, using porcelainlike figures.

The Nightingale. Translated by Naomi Lewis and illustrated by Josef Palacek. North-South, 1990. Lovely jewel-toned paintings emphasize the strong emotions in this tale.

The Nightingale. Translated by Anthea Bell; illustrated by Lisbeth Zwerger. Picturebook Studio, 1984. The pale tones used, primarily gray-blue and taupe, give a lighter, almost ethereal, quality to the story.

Solo Pantomime Activities

Pantomime Solo

- Everyone is hurriedly getting the palace ready for the appearance of the nightingale. There is much cleaning and polishing to be done and there is much scurrying to and fro. What will your special task be and how will you carry it out? Remember that everything in the palace is very fragile and exquisite. As I play the music, you work rapidly and efficiently, but carefully.

- You are the music master, writing the "five-and-twenty" volumes about the artificial bird in Chinese characters. You'll need to work very fast in order to accomplish the task. As I play the music, let us see you working feverishly to explain everything you have to say about this most unusual bird. (*Play fast music or a selection at fast speed.*)

Narrative Pantomime

- You are the emperor on your death bed. Death is like a heavy weight on your chest and you can scarcely breathe. The nightingale comes and sings its comforting songs, and slowly the weight lifts. The blood courses through your veins, giving strength to your feeble body. Slowly, very slowly, you rise from your bed and stand with renewed strength, ready to greet the new day.

Solo Verbal Activities

Verbal Solo

- (*You may question and respond as the emperor's servant.*) All those who have heard the nightingale sing say it is the loveliest sound they have ever heard. The kitchen maid told us it brought tears to her eyes and she felt as if her mother were kissing her. You who have heard this nightingale sing, how would you describe it?

- Music master, explain the differences you notice in the real nightingale's song and the mechanical nightingale's song.

- Little nightingale, why did you fly away from the palace after the mechanical bird came? Where did you go—and why that particular place? And how did you know the emperor needed you and that he was dying?

- You are the emperor of Japan who sent the mechanical bird to the emperor of China. What was your reason for doing that and for including this note that reads, "The emperor of Japan's nightingale is very poor, compared with the emperor of China's"?

- You're the watchmaker who was finally able to repair the mechanical nightingale. Could you tell us what was wrong with it, how you repaired it, and what condition it's in now?

- The little nightingale offers to sing to the emperor of many things— the happy, the thoughtful. In fact, as long as the emperor tells no one, the nightingale will be a little bird that tells the emperor everything that he sees, being free to fly about the entire kingdom. What one thing might the little bird know—something the emperor might not be aware of, isolated as he is in the palace? You're the nightingale. Tell us.

Paired and Group Pantomime Activities

Tug of War

- The emperor's good and bad deeds struggle against each other.

Frozen Pictures

- The emperor and his court are listening to the nightingale sing at its first command performance. Show by your bodies and faces how they would react to its rare and wonderful sounds. (*Use groups of six.*)

- Select your favorite scene to show.

Improvised Scene

- Let us see the nightingale on one of its outings with the footmen. Don't forget the ribbons tied to the nightingale's little leg. Show where you think they go on the outing and also what you think happens or what everyone does when they all return to the palace. (*Use groups of seven.*)

- Show death visiting the dying emperor, and the entrance, one by one, of all the faces of the emperor's good and bad deeds. Remember, some are hideous while others are gentle and pleasant. Show the emperor's reaction. After the nightingale sings its comfort and hope, the emperor's reaction will change, causing death and the deeds to depart. (*Try groups of eight to include the emperor, death, and three each of the good and bad deeds. Suggest that death and the good and bad deeds move in slow motion. Rather than miming the nightingale, perhaps some sound effect could be used to show its entrance. Play slow music throughout.*)

Mechanical Movement

- Suppose the mechanical nightingale was admired so much that the emperor ordered a large-sized imitation to be made. In groups of six, create your version of this invention. As music plays, you will move as the bird might have moved as it sang. (*Use mechanical-sounding music or have students create sound effects and do this as a sound mime.*)

Paired and Group Verbal Activities

Sound Effects

- The flowers in the emperor's garden are extraordinarily beautiful and have little silver bells tied to them. As one walks through the garden, they tinkle perpetually, enticing you to look at them. Let's create that sound. First a gentle breeze, then the tinkling, silver bells. (*The breeze may be vocal; the bells will probably have to be mechanically produced. Experiment with found objects around the classroom.*)

Conversation

- (*Divide the class into groups of five.*) The sound of the nightingale becomes so fashionable the courtiers try to imitate its voice by filling their mouths with water. Talk about the sensation the nightingale is creating as the courtiers might have sounded. When I call your group's number, let's hear a little of your conversation. (*Although children might think they need water to do this activity, challenge them to do it using the art of pretense. After all, anyone could do it with water; a real actor can do it without!*)

- When the courtiers discover the real nightingale has flown away, they are upset with its ingratitude. What are some of the things they might be saying? (*Use groups of five.*)

- (*Use groups of four.*) The emperor's good and bad deeds whisper to him, one after the other, reminding him of all the things he had done in the past. Make a list of some of the things that might have been said, alternating the good and the bad. Keep each idea to just one sentence. Then, when I call your group's number, you will take turns whispering your list of deeds. (*Encourage the children to overlap their ideas so they flow menacingly. Try increasing the volume of whispering as another way to enhance the tension. You might also be death, nodding your head, as he did, while the deeds speak.*)

- (*Do after the above activity, still with groups of four.*) While the good and bad deeds reminded the emperor of his past, the emperor tried to shut them out with his own thoughts. Write out what these thoughts might have been. Again, keep them all to just one sentence each. This time when I call your group's number, you will be speaking aloud as the emperor.

Debate

- (*Do after the above activity, but change to groups of five.*) Now, two will be the good deeds, two the bad deeds, and one will be the emperor. As I point to your group, the good and bad deeds will tell the emperor what he doesn't want to hear while he counters with his thoughts in an attempt to silence them.

- After the mechanical nightingale breaks, the emperor calls in his personal physicians to examine it. The emperor is distraught and feels the physicians should be able to cure the artificial nightingale since they are some of the most learned men in the kingdom; the physicians must persuade the emperor that other measures are needed. (*Do in groups of three.*)

- Some people in the kingdom feel the real nightingale has the most beautiful voice; others feel there are advantages to the mechanical nightingale. What various reasons are presented? (*Divide the class in half. You moderate the discussion as a neutral person, not sure which side to believe.*)

Sound Mime

- (*Do in pairs.*) The jeweled nightingale is mechanical, like a windup toy, and sings waltzes. One of you will be the nightingale, the other will sing its song. Windup toys often start fast and get slower as they wind down, stopping sometimes in midsong. Consider this as you plan.

- Repeat the above, but this time the mechanical nightingale breaks down completely.

Leader in Role

- (*You play the emperor's gentleman in waiting.*) Councilors, I have called you together to decide an appropriate gift to send to the emperor of Japan in return for the beautiful, jeweled bird he sent our emperor. This will not be an easy decision. The gift must be equal in beauty. Whatever it is, it must not offend in any way. We are counting on you to suggest something that will give further glory to our emperor. I shall return in a while to hear your ideas. (*Use groups of five.*)

- (*You play an official of the kingdom.*) Our beloved emperor, as you know, is at death's door. Let us remember the many things about him, the things he did, that made him so dear to us all. Let each one in turn tell what one thing you will remember most about him. Who would like to begin?

- (*You play an official of the kingdom.*) My fellow councilors, I'm grieved to tell you that our emperor is gravely ill. While we will certainly feel a very deep loss at his passing, we must also prepare for the future. We will be selecting a new emperor very shortly, so it is imperative that we consider the qualifications we want in our ruler. Please discuss this among yourselves, make your list of qualifications, and then number them in the order of their importance to you. I shall return to hear your considerations after a while.

Related Activities

- The jeweled nightingale was considered so superior to the real nightingale that the latter was banished from the kingdom. In groups, you are the emperor's councilors, writing out the banishment decree. When you have finished, you will read it aloud to the public.

- The emperor of China first learned about the nightingale through poems and descriptions written about it. Prepare poems or other descriptions praising the beauty of the nightingale. As an alternative, look for poems and descriptions other writers have penned about birds.

- Although this is not a Chinese folktale, do further research on the customs and culture of China referred to in the story. Integrate them into the drama when appropriate.

- Suppose the emperor in the story had died. What kind of funeral would there have been? What similarities and differences would there be to funeral services we are familiar with? (*Children may even wish to dramatize a funeral ceremony for an emperor.*)

- Examine some Chinese characters and pictographs used in writing. Create your own pictographs.

- Pretend to be the music master writing his impressions of the nightingale. Incorporate some of the pictographs you've studied or created.

- Make face masks for the good and bad deeds. (*Use sturdy paper plates with tongue depressors attached as handles.*)

- Design a garden with drawings and landscape plans, suitable for a palace.

- Listen to recordings of bird songs. Compare the nightingale's song with the songs of other birds.

The Pied Piper of Hamelin

ROBERT BROWNING

Summary: *When the town of Hamelin is inundated with rats, a curious stranger offers to get rid of them for a thousand guilders. By playing haunting music on his pipe, he entices them into the sea, where they all—save one—drown. But when the town refuses to pay the piper for his services, he entices all the children through a magical door in a mountain's side, where they are forever lost. One lame child, who could not keep up with the rest, is left to tell the story.*

Selected Picture Books

The Pied Piper of Hamelin. Written by Robert Browning and illustrated by Anatoly Ivanov. Lothrup, Lee and Shepard, 1986. Rich color and fine details make this an impressive rendition.

The Pied Piper of Hamelin. Retold by Sara and Stephen Corrin and illustrated by Errol LeCain. Harcourt, Brace, 1989. Detailed illustrations, emphasizing earthtones, show particularly expressive faces.

The Pied Piper of Hamelin. Retold and illustrated by Mercer Mayer. Macmillan, 1987. The illustrations place the viewer at ground level, which lends to the oppressive feeling of the tale. In this version, the children go to a better and happier place.

The Pied Piper of Hamelin. Retold and illustrated by Tony Ross. Lothrop, Lee and Shepard, 1977. An upbeat ending and cartoon-style drawings present a happier mood than is usual for this story.

Solo Pantomime Activities

Pantomime Solo

- Rats are everywhere in Hamelin town. You are a citizen trying to do your daily work, but you run into rats at every turn. As you pantomime three tasks you do during your day, at least one rat will interrupt your work in some way. When I ring the bell, begin working. When you discover the rat, freeze in horror. (*Do three times.*)

- Be the pied piper playing your pipe for the rats, feeling successful because this secret charm of yours will garner a thousand guilders. Now be the pied piper playing your pipe for the children, expressing feelings of revenge over the way the city officials treated you.

Solo Verbal Activities

Verbal Solo

- Pretend that you are either the one rat who survived or the lame child who was left behind. Describe for us what it felt like to be so attracted to the piper's music. What did the music say you would find if you followed it?

- You are the mayor of the town. Tell us, how do you think the situation with the rats got so out of hand? Who do you blame?

- You're the piper. How did you hear about the troubles of this town? Where were you and what were you doing at the time?

Paired and Group Pantomime Activities

Frozen Picture

- The rats drowning in the Weser River.
- The children joyfully following the pied piper.
- The parents desperately trying to penetrate the walled mountain to retrieve their lost children.

Paired and Group Verbal Activities

Leader in Role

- (*You play the mayor.*) Thank you for appearing here today. You know the difficulty we're in and that we're in desperate need of your expert services. I'd like for you to work in groups of five and develop a list of ideas for getting rid of the rats (*e.g., chemical warfare, various designs of rat traps*). I need to meet with the council on some other matters, but will return shortly. At that time you will select your group's best idea to explain and demonstrate. (*You may stipulate that only environmentally safe solutions will be acceptable to the council.*)

• In small groups, be a public relations team for the mayor and the town corporation. The pied piper has had his revenge, and you have to write and then deliver an official statement from the city government for the news media. How will you explain the events so the city officials will look good to the citizens? (*You play the mayor.*)

• The text mentions that after the children were taken away, a street, Pied Piper Street, was dedicated; the story was written on a column; and a church window depicted the event. In what other ways might the children be honored? In small groups discuss your plans for a memorial to the lost children. Enact your memorial ceremony. (*Materials can be made available for construction of memorial wreaths, plaques, or other remembrances. Appropriate music may also be added to the ceremony. You organize as the mayor.*)

Sound Effects

• The rats shriek and squeak "in fifty different sharps and flats." On cue, let's hear the sounds of the rats. (*Do in small groups. If it appears feasible, combine the groups one at a time.*)

• When the pied piper played his music for the rats, "you heard as if an army muttered; and the muttering grew to a grumbling; and the grumbling grew to a mighty rumbling. . . . " Recreate these sounds, escalating to the mighty rumble. (*Begin with a few children and add sounds to create the increasing intensity. This should be an impressive, low rumbling rather than loud sounds.*)

• When the pied piper played his music for the children, there were rustling and bustling, pattering feet, wooden shoes clattering, little hands clapping, and little tongues chattering. In your groups, you will be responsible for one of the sounds I assign you. Group one will start and the others will join in when I point to you until you all are making sounds together.

Interview

• The mayor interviews the mysterious pied piper. What is the job description? What qualifications, references, and previous job experiences can be presented? Shake hands when you reach your agreement. (*May be played in pairs, or the leader may pretend to be the mayor.*)

- (*Do in pairs.*) You are the two survivors, the lame child and the one rat. Compare the similarities and differences of your experiences with the pied piper—the sound of the music, the way it drew you along, and so on. (*These may be written down and discussed with whole class afterward.*)

Debate

- Half the class will be the townspeople of Hamelin, who descend upon the mayor and the corporation (*the other half*) and rail at them for spending money foolishly and doing nothing about the rats. The mayor and the corporation try to defend their behaviors and expenditures of money. (*You may be a secretary taking notes.*)

- After the pied piper's revenge, the parents meet with the mayor and the town corporation and demand that the piper be paid and the children returned, or else. The officials try to excuse themselves and calm the parents. (*Divide the class in half; you play the role of the town secretary taking notes.*)

- The children have been gone for some time. Many parents and relatives are still in mourning for them; others are beginning to think there are advantages to living in a community with no children. The two sides discuss the pros and cons of this issue.

Related Activities

- What information about this legend can you find in other sources? Collect the theories and compare them. Which sounds like the most plausible explanation?

- Draw a picture of the pleasant sights the pied piper's tune said the children would see behind the portals to the mountain.

- Write an entry in the rat's diary of the day he escaped drowning with all his relatives in the Weser River.

- Consider the expression "pay the piper" or "pay the piper his due." What does it mean?

- Construct the financial ledger for the town, before, during, and after the pied piper's visit. What story does it tell?

The Search for Thor's Hammer

A Norse Myth

Summary: *Thor, the strongest of the gods, has a wonderfully powerful hammer that is stolen by the mighty giant Thrym. Loki, god of the underworld and prime suspect, establishes his innocence and gets Thrym to confess. Thrym promises to give the hammer back if the gods will send the beautiful Freia to be his bride. The malicious prankster Loki persuades Thor to dress as a woman and go in Freia's place. Reluctantly, Thor carries out the plan, retrieves his hammer, and kills Thrym with it.*

Sources

"The Quest of the Hammer." Written by Abbie Farwell Brown. From *In the Days of Giants*. Houghton Mifflin, 1902. From *Stories to Dramatize* by Winifred Ward. Anchorage, 1981.

"The Theft of Thor's Hammer." Written by Ingri and Edgar D'Aulaire. From *D'Aulaires' Norse Gods and Giants*. Doubleday, 1967.

Solo Pantomime Activities

Pantomime Solo

- As the music plays you will be Loki or Freia, dressed in the magic falcon feathers, flying about the world. As the music draws to a close, you will end your flight. (*Students may fly around their desks individually or in a space made around all the desks. Depending on space available, you may need to work in small groups. For music you might use Wagner's "Ride of the Valkyries."*)

129

Narrative Pantomime

- You will be Thor the Thunderer awakening in the morning. You will yawn, stretch, and slip your hand under your pillow of clouds to grasp your precious hammer, Miölnir. But the hammer will have disappeared! As I count to five, (*silently and in slow motion*) you will let out a roar of rage that shakes the entire palace. When I say "Freeze," you will put your head in your hands and gather your thoughts about what to do about this miserable event. (*You will sidecoach during the activity as needed.*)

- You are Thor, angrily and feverishly searching for the hammer among the clouds of Thrudheim. You look in every corner, tossing the clouds about like pillows, and set them to rolling in the heavens. All is in vain. The hammer is nowhere to be found.

- You are Thor, pretending to be Freia, eating at the banquet the giants have prepared for you. Under the veil covering your face, you stuff pieces of a whole roast ox. This is followed by eight pink salmon and an entire platter of cakes and sweet meats intended for the women guests. Finally you wash it all down with three barrels of mead, the foamy drink of the giants. Thank goodness your hunger and thirst are finally satisfied. Now, stifle that belch and, for the sake of this deceit, try to compose yourself!

- You are Thrym, throwing the hammer to make thunder like Thor. But you aren't as skillful as he, and you're creating a wild tempest. As I count to five, you will throw the hammer five times, once for each count. Try a different throwing technique each time in your impossible effort to imitate Thor.

- You are Thor or Loki, dressed in a woman's wedding gown, practicing walking and sitting so as not to stumble. Hold the train of your gown over one arm. Now try walking around your chair. Now pretend to go up a flight of six steps and back down. Now try to sit gracefully on your chair. Too bad we don't have a longer time to practice. I guess this will have to do.

Solo Verbal Activities

Verbal Solo

- You are Thrym. It's really remarkable that you were able to steal the hammer from Thor while it was under his cloud pillow as he slept. Let us hear about your clever theft. How did you accomplish it?

- You are Heimdal, the sleepless watchman who guards the entrance to the rainbow bridge leading to Asgard. Tell about your plan to have Thor dress as Freia. Remember you are speaking through your golden teeth that you are probably proud of and like to show off.

- Suppose Loki tries another trick with Thor and suggests that he has a better hammer to give him. You are Loki. Tell us what this new hammer will be like and how it will be superior to the first one.

- You are Thrym, with a terrible voice you proudly *think* is as powerful as Thor's. Call out your greeting to Loki as he approaches you outside your palace.

Noiseless Sound

- You are Loki. Thor has threatened to punish you if you laugh at him. But just the thought of this whole episode can send you into gales of laughter. Let's see what happens when Thor has his back turned to you and then suddenly turns to watch you. You must stifle all sounds at all times. (*You might sketch a face on a piece of cardboard and turn it to cue Thor's watching of and turning from Loki. Try this perhaps three times to practice. Then let small groups share their interpretations of this activity with the rest of the class.*)

Paired and Group Pantomime Activities

Tug of War

- Suppose the Norse gods are having a tug of war with their enemies, the giants. Who will win today? Or will it be an even match?

Build a Place

- Thrym wants to impress his bride-to-be with the amount of his treasure. He calls for his servants to make his house beautiful and to show off his possessions. What are some of the things they might bring in?

- You are the cooks, laying out the huge wedding feast on the long banquet table. From the way you make the final preparations of each food item and carry it to the table we will try to guess what it is.

Pantomime Spelling

- Spell out the names of the characters in the story, recognizing that there are variations for some of them (e.g., Freya; Freia).

Frozen Picture

• Create a series of three frozen pictures. The first will be the aftermath of Thor's first throw of the hammer, which kills Thrym; after the second throw, the whole giant household is killed; after the third throw, the entire palace is in ruins. (*Use groups of eight, nine, or ten. You might wish to do all three pictures together as a slow-motion scene.*)

Improvised Scene

• (*Use groups of four.*) Thor is being dressed as a bride by the women. The women are amused to see the mighty Thor submitting to what he feels is a disgraceful state, and they joke and snicker to themselves behind his back. As they approach him to help in the disguise, however, they put on serious faces so as not to offend him. First, they fit and sew his clothes, then do his hair, and finish with the veil to hide his face. He insists on wearing his iron gloves, however.

Paired and Group Verbal Activities

Conversation

• The women giants at the banquet table are astonished to see the "bride" eat so much food, including the dessert intended for them. They whisper among themselves, worried that a queen with such an appetite could mean less food for them at all future meals. What might they say? (*Use groups of four, five, or six.*)

• The people in the land of the frost giants are troubled over Thrym's choice of a bride. They wonder why he is not satisfied to choose one of the women in his own land as his wife. Why is it necessary, they wonder, to bring someone from another kingdom? Let us hear some of this discussion as they talk. (*Do in groups of five.*)

• Suppose that when Thor asks his wife, Sif, to assist him in searching for the hammer, she admonishes him for always losing things. How might this conversation sound as Thor and Sif try in vain to find the hammer?

Debate

• The palace servants are not in agreement. Half of them are against Freia's having to marry the ugly frost giant and live in his dreadful kingdom, Jotunheim, where it is always winter. On the other side are those who say that Loki's word to Thrym must be kept and that Thor needs his powerful hammer to protect them from their enemies. Let us hear some of this debate.

- Again the palace servants are in disagreement. Half of them think Thor should go along with Heimdal's plan of dressing up like a bride. The other half think the whole idea is disgraceful. Let us hear some of their reasoning.

Leader in Role

- (*You play Thor.*) As you know, I have a hammer that is very important to me and to my kingdom. Since it has been stolen once, it could be stolen again. What advice can you give me about its safekeeping? (*This activity will be more successful if the students keep in mind Thor's position and size as well as his relationship to other characters in the story.*)

Improvised Scene

- Let us hear the scene that takes place when Thor confronts Loki regarding the theft of the hammer. Loki maintains his innocence and implicates Thrym. Remember that Loki mumbles because his lips are still sore from having been stitched up during his last mischievous adventure.

- Thrym tries to welcome his "bride" and make her feel at home in his kingdom. But he is beginning to wonder about her strange mannerisms, the amount of food she eats, her silence, and the glaring looks he sees flashing under her veil. He questions Loki, dressed as a bridesmaid, about her behavior. Loki must try to keep Thrym from discovering the "bride's" and his own true identity. He must also keep the impatient Thor from giving away the disguise too soon. Let us see some of this scene and the predicament Loki finds himself in.

Who Am I?

- Pretend to be the various gods and giants in the story.

Related Activities

- Read other adventures of Thor, both before and after the story of the stolen hammer. What information learned from these stories makes the characters in this story more understandable?

- Write a diary account, from Loki's perspective, of what happened in the story. No doubt he will make himself the hero.

- Thor rides a goat-drawn chariot whose rolling wheels make the sound of thunder. A thunderbolt occurs when his hammer flies back into his hand. What beliefs about natural weather occurrences can be found in other myths?

- Loki promises never to tell about Thor's dressing up as a bride. But the story is known today. So, who told it? Write a story explaining how this legend came to be known.

- Thor's Day has become our Thursday. How did this come about? What information can be discovered about the other days of the week?

BIBLIOGRAPHY

Best-Loved Folk-Tales of the World. Selected by Joanna Cole. Doubleday, 1982. Contains versions of twelve of the tales in this book.

The Brothers Grimm. Translated by Brian Alderson. Illustrated by Michael Foreman. Doubleday, 1978. Contains "Briar Rose," "Snow White," "Frog King," "Hansel and Gretel," and "Rumplestiltskin."

Cinderella and Other Tales from Perrault. Illustrated by Michael Hague. Henry Holt, 1989. Includes "Sleeping Beauty," "Cinderella," and "Little Red Riding Hood."

Into the Woods. Stephen Sondheim and James Lapine. Adapted and illustrated by Hudson Talbott. Crown, 1988. A retelling of the popular Broadway stage show in which the lives of fairy tale characters impact on one another. An intriguing blend of traditional and modern interpretations of the stories is presented.

The Jolly Postman. Janet and Allan Ahlberg. Little, Brown, 1986. A collection of imaginative letters sent to and from people in favorite tales. The pages are envelopes with facsimiles of letters tucked inside. Stories referred to include "Cinderella," "The Three Bears," "Jack and the Beanstalk," "Hansel and Gretel," and "Little Red Riding Hood."

The Riverside Anthology of Children's Literature. Sixth edition. Edited by Judith Saltman. Houghton Mifflin, 1985. All the stories used in this book may be found in this anthology.

Roald Dahl's Revolting Rhymes. Roald Dahl. Illustrated by Quentin Blake. Knopf, 1983. Favorite fairy tales retold with humor, brashness, and even some violence.

Stories to Dramatize. Edited by Winifred Ward. Anchorage, 1981. Includes "The Three Billy Goats Gruff," "Goldilocks and the Three Bears," "Cinderella," "Rumplestiltskin," "The Sleeping Beauty," "Snow White and the Seven Dwarfs," and "The Quest of the Hammer."

Story Hour. Sara Henderson Hay. Illustrated by Jim McMollan. Double-
    day, 1963. A collection of poems that give new and rather sophisti-
    cated interpretations and insights into the folktales.

The Three Princesses: Cinderella, Sleeping Beauty, Snow White. Compiled by
    Cooper Edens. Bantam, 1991. Includes notes on the historical back-
    ground of the stories as well as selected illustrations from many
    classical editions of the past one hundred and twenty five years.